"It has been an absolute joy to care for Ross and watch him grow up into such an extraordinary young man. His academic and social achievements are an inspiration to all of my autistic patients and offer real hope to families of these children everywhere."
– Joseph J. DelGiorno, M.D.

"A MUST READ for any parent...but especially for parents of children diagnosed with autism. Linda integrates so many great tips, techniques and strategies into a warm and loving story about a boy...about a family...and about autism! Although Linda, her family, friends, and all those fabulous educators and therapists referred to have contributed to Ross' life, it is Ross who has "touched" all of their lives! Having been one of the privileged professionals who worked with Ross, I can say how much I learned from this gentle soul and from his honesty, humor and great view of life. He taught me so much more about "high functioning autism" than any book or course available. I say thank you for letting me be part of the process and the receiver of joy and having the privilege of watching you grow as a family and allowing me to witness the amazing transformation of Ross into a wonderful young man. This is a marvelous book and journey for all parents to read. Enjoy and learn from it!"
– Edward G. Daniels, PA Licensed Psychologist, PA/NJ Certified School Psychologist.

"I highly recommend "Beating the Odds at Autism," a wonderful testimonial of one family's trials and triumphs as they address the impact of autism in their lives. The Burns family is gracious to share their personal experience, as it will undoubtedly inspire others and offer practical advice to families who struggle with profound challenges. Although this is a story about Autism, I think most families who adopt the Burns' winning attitude can overcome their own difficulties, regardless of the source, with humor, meaningful actions and the love and support of those around them."
– Dr. Kathleen McCabe-Odri, BCBA-D.

"This book delivers a powerful message to parents and professionals alike about how sensory processing problems may affect attention, learning and behavior of a child. The reader will gain valuable insight into simple, yet effective strategies to help minimize anxiety and meltdowns. One of the reasons Ross is the wonderful young man that he is today is because he has many sensory strategies which keep his nervous system in that "just right place" to deal with life's challenges."

– Jenny Sammons, Master of Science in Occupational Therapy.

"I am far from an expert on autism, but I know when something is working correctly...and what Ross and his family are doing is working correctly. When Ross first came to us, I was told of his condition and really did not see any concern on our part. He fit in and the players really rallied around him. As the years progressed, so did Ross. His confidence grew and by the time he was a senior it was like he never even had autism. As we say in football, there are 101 ways to do something. You just need to find ONE of those 101 ways of doing something and BELIEVE IN IT. I believe that the plan and strategies that Linda and her family chose is one of those ways."

– Mark Wechter, RKC, Health and Physical Education teacher – Head Football Coach, Washington Township High School.

Beating the Odds at Autism

One Family's Winning Hand

Linda, Ashley and Ross Burns

Foreword by Jenn Reges, LICSW

Photography by Dennis Kelly and Lori Belmonte

Copyright © 2012 by Linda, Ashley and Ross Burns
Photography by Dennis Kelly & Lori Belmonte

ISBN 978-0-7414-7088-1 Color Paperback
ISBN 978-0-7414-7472-8 Paperback
ISBN 978-0-7414-7089-8 eBook
Library of Congress Control Number: 2011943686

Printed in the United States of America

Published October 2012

Follow us on Facebook, Twitter and LinkedIn

INFINITY PUBLISHING

Toll-free (877) BUY BOOK
Local Phone (610) 941-9999
Fax (610) 941-9959
Info@buybooksontheweb.com
www.buybooksontheweb.com

Contents

To My Son, thank you for teaching me to find something to be thankful for every day. I hope you'll always "feel" how much I love you...

Acknowledgments

"The only real valuable thing is intuition."

Albert Einstein

I believe to succeed in life...whether it is successfully bringing a child who is born with autism to their full potential or whatever the definition of success may mean to you...it takes a visionary with a creative mind, a whole lot of passion and commitment, and a touch of intuition. It also takes surrounding yourself with the proper people and the willingness to allow them to support you. I hope as you read on that you'll gain a glimpse at what was essential to me as a parent of a child with autism and apply it, if appropriate, to any given situation that may be challenging in your lifetime.

And now I want to extend my most sincere gratitude to the many individuals who have touched my family so deeply, in so many ways, and who have become part of my life forever.

The only place to start is at the beginning, so to my family who always tried to understand and be supportive...even when we didn't yet have a diagnosis...and with whom I couldn't have survived those volatile years. To my parents, who were living in Naples, Florida during most of Ross' childhood and offered to move back if I were to just say the words. To my sister's family, who opened their home to sleepovers as a way of offering some respite. Yes, even to my uncle, who "affectionately" nicknamed me "Mommy Dearest" because of my relentless adherence to the rules of conduct! To my niece, who attempted to learn all she could in an effort to be there for me. To my cousins, who embraced my family situation and made it their own.

And then on to our initial consultant, Dr. Kathleen McCabe-Odri, BCBA-D and her team who came into my home for a three-day workshop and set the groundwork for a lifetime of success...and a hell of a lot of hard work and commitment. Her advanced knowledge (especially 17 years ago), experience and brilliance that she brought to Ross' unique program provided the hope and motivation that we needed to get rolling. And every tutor/therapist who has ever walked through our door: Lori (our dark horse – you hit the ground running!)... Jacqueline, Audrey, Stephanie, Jenn, Claudia (all of you at one time or another have stood in my foyer -- tears in our eyes -- after an emotionally-draining session)... Linda, Chris, Susan, and all of the other part-timers...thanks for all of your love and commitment. And then to Lori P. Candon, M.Ed., LDTC, BCBA ...your insight and fresh perspective during Ross' teen years proved invaluable. To Ed Daniels, PA/NJ Certified School Psychologist, whose strong yet reassuring male influence sustained Ross through those difficult teenage years.

To the administrators from Washington Township School District, especially Pat, Kimberly and Pam, who from the inception, were able to convey a sense of comfort. I never took the rapport that we had for granted. These administrators would sit tirelessly around my kitchen table every other week, listen attentively, offer suggestions, and then trust and believe in my sometimes "unconventional" suggestions and ideas...I thank you for believing in me. To every teacher whose door Ross has ever entered...from his initial teacher and aide in the preschool program...right up until his professors and advisors at Gloucester County College. I've had the privilege of working with professionals who were able to embrace our program when, at times, perhaps not fully understanding the depth of it...as many of them never aspired to become "special education" teachers but now found children like Ross mainstreamed into their regular education classrooms. I want to thank every principal and guidance counselor who listened to our strategies and allowed us to implement them in their classrooms...and hopefully as a result set an example for what a structured ABA home/school program should look like in order to reap its benefits.

My thanks to Ross' team of physicians and neurologists who helped track and guide his physical and mental wellness.

To our many friends, who not only helped nurture Ross' friendships with their sons and daughters, but really tried to understand the difficult behaviors that sometimes surfaced...which was not easy because at times we didn't understand them...but hung in there in an effort to be a good friend. You'll always have a special place in my heart. To my dear friends, who not being parents at the time, took on a superhuman understanding of what I, as a mother, was going through and never made me feel like our worlds were polar opposite. To my hair stylist and friend, who upon learning of this book, gave me inspiration by telling me..."be yourself and write the book as you're talking to me right now over a cup of coffee...that's what will touch the hearts of readers."

To my clients and court reporters, most of whom I have known since Ross was diagnosed and who have acted as quasi therapists for me at times...whether you've listened attentively or offered advice...it didn't go unnoticed. For always making me feel that ours was more than a client relationship, I am forever grateful.

To Bill, Lucy and Justin...my heartfelt gratitude for your support and guidance through this book writing and editing process: Bill, for the endless research regarding publishing that you threw yourself into and your attention to detail; Lucy, for your impeccable knowledge and adherence to rules and your efforts to keep my wandering mind in check; and to Justin, for managing to navigate through my off-the-wall requests and somehow figuring out how to make them "appear in print."

To the two guys in my life...my husband Bob and my son Ross...who have taught me so much about patience, understanding and unconditional love. I've learned a lot about relationships...and what's really important in relationships...while going through this journey with the two of you as bookends!

And lastly...to my daughter Ashley who has been my strength over the years...even at a young age. Her poise, grace and resilience have carried me through the tough days and I continue to learn from her as she is

Beating the Odds at Autism

now embarking on the second phase of her life...one in which she will continue to reach out and be a source of strength and guidance for those who struggle...just as she has always been for her brother (and her mom!) I could not have imagined this journey without you, My Dear Ashley.

Preface

    Here I sit on the beach on an August day and instead of proofreading deposition transcripts, I decide to begin this book. People have always said that getting started is the hardest part; however, for me, where to start was more of a challenge. I think one of the most important things to consider when writing a book...not that I've had experience...is deciding who your target audience will be. For me, this is threefold since my son Ross will be giving his personal and paramount perspective on things; my daughter Ashley will lend her personal accounts as a sibling, and I will share mine as a mom, confidant, teacher, friend, advocate, and a multitude of other hats that I've worn over the years.

    So, I guess what I've decided is, I hope that this book touches the hearts of many...the myriad of children, teens and young adults living with the challenges that autism presents; siblings who have had their childhood turned upside down to accommodate endless demands; and parents whom I wish to inspire with insight, experiential knowledge and hope. I've decided not to elaborate on the definition of autism because, thanks to the internet, books written by parents, educators and PhDs, and heightened awareness by organizations like Autism Speaks, most are cognizant of what autism is and how its symptoms and behaviors manifest themselves. I use the term symptoms because I truly believe that the behaviors are symptoms of the spectrum disorder which can be minimized, channeled and even eliminated in some cases through behavior modification, self-motivation and a strong constitution...and I don't want to leave out a hell of a lot of hard work!

A term you'll not hear me use in this book is disability as a standalone without linking it with learning...and then it will be followed by a suggested intervention, treatment or therapy. While I realize and recommend that labels and classifications should be given in the educational setting to avail your son or daughter to all of the services, therapies, and modifications available, they are only labels and should never "cap off" an individual's capabilities. Try to maximize your child's strengths and you'll soon be celebrating more and more accomplishments. Continuously set goals and raise that bar according to your child's successes. Don't ever rest, be content or stop searching for avenues to take your child to that next level. You will, at times, be surprised; however, always pleased with the results. Our children never, ever cease to amaze us and after all these years I continue to learn on a daily basis new things about, not only autism, but about my son! These children give the phrase "work in progress" new meaning!

As I sit here today looking out into the ocean, I have to say that the answers were never written in the sand as I would take my long walks over the years with Ross holding my hand, or even found in books, or by sitting around my kitchen table twice a month with consultants,

Beating the Odds at Autism

teachers, tutors and Child Study Team members. Sometimes the answers came to light from my gut feelings; my intuition. Suggestions would be made by "the best of the best" in their field, which is how I've viewed the professionals who I've had the honor to be surrounded by...but no one knows your child like you do. Please remember that. So I would ask that you try to be receptive to ideas or strategies laid out in this book and be flexible in, perhaps, adapting them to your child's functioning level. Because the one thing we do know about autism is that every child is different and unique. There is no classic definition of autism in my eyes, and I feel that's what makes the syndrome so intriguing in ways you could never imagine. Frustrating at times...but nonetheless intriguing!

I feel that upfront, the proper thing to do would be to apologize if Ross, or Ashley, or I offend anyone in our writings. We may take strong stands on some issues; all the while attempting to bring humor to this very serious topic. I personally attribute the ability to laugh essential in dealing with life's challenges and Ross especially shares my sense of humor. It's hard to feel defeat, loneliness or sadness when you're laughing! And as I've often said to those close to me...with all of the sadness in my life, I am not sad.

Ross never wanted to be treated differently, so he's worked harder than any adult I know to achieve many of his goals. But I've always told him, "Keep the parts of autism that make you the amazing person that you are and the person I am so proud to call My Son."

So...now that I've gotten that off my chest...my wish for our readers is that you be open-minded and lighthearted while truly getting a glimpse into "a day in the life" in the world of autism!

Preface

Foreword

In preparing to write this foreword, I asked myself again and again, "How can I best introduce the complex and wonderful Ross Burns?" I think in part I'll need to introduce him in the context of his parents and his older sister as they played such crucial and positive roles in the development of who Ross has become. This is not to say that Ross himself is not due immense credit for his own growth; indeed, I have yet to meet another student with as much perseverance and resilience as Ross.

I worked with Ross from the time he was 7 to 12 years old and I was 20 to 25. I was pursuing my Bachelors in Psychology at Rowan University and thought that working with a boy who had autism would help to make real some of what I was learning. What I didn't realize was that – over time – it would also grant me additional family members. Within a couple of years, Ross and his sister Ashley started to consider me their "cousin" and Ross' Dad Bob began calling me his "long-lost oldest daughter." For this role I took on the alias

"Allyson" (always with a y) and this name and family understanding has continued to this day.

Ross knew I was the discrete trial facilitator who came on "T days" – Tuesdays and Thursdays. I believe the hours were from 4 to 7 pm. Another woman (who has also had the pleasure of becoming an adopted family member) worked with Ross on Monday and Wednesday evenings. He would arrive home from school, enjoy a snack, and then get right back to work. With breaks provided occasionally, we focused on one discrete trial after another. Some of the goals included increasing reading comprehension, decoding idioms, and accurately perceiving social situations via the use of role plays and social stories. Ashley – very willingly and lovingly – would join us during some of these sessions and served as a junior facilitator who modeled positive social behaviors and effective communication skills. Some of our most productive work was done with Ashley's gentle and astute assistance. She remains a perceptive, compassionate role model and an amazing support to Ross.

Whether it was within the discrete trials or around the kitchen table, focus was continuously placed on communication and social skills building. During family dinners, for example, all of us would discuss our "highs" and "lows" of the day. This was a concrete, routine communication pattern that not only helped Ross participate in conversation, but helped the family to connect and support each other. The remainder of Ross' weeknights consisted of completing homework, attending karate classes, and maybe watching a bit of television. To say Ross is a hard worker seems a gross understatement. On all of those "T days" and in the many years that have passed since, Ross has shown an incredibly determined spirit. He rarely complained, seeming to know deep down that all of his work came with worthwhile payoffs.

A year or two after I stopped working with Ross, Linda told me some professionals believed that his diagnosis should be changed to Asperger's Syndrome. Until this time, he was considered to have autism and to be "high-functioning." The discrete trial work continued, but Ross went about it (and life) with improved communication skills and social abilities. Ross himself would refer to his diagnosis as 'the A word,' and, as the process of diagnosing can be quite murky, I think this suffices.

For someone whose disability was supposed to render him somewhat asocial, it was amazing to observe and experience the ways in which Ross would socially engage and would socially connect. For example, one afternoon when we were starting to get to work, Ross asked me, "Jenn, why do you always say 'so' before you say something? You say 'so Ross.' Why do you say 'so'?" I think he was 10 at the time and very communicatively on point! I remember thinking how extraordinary it was for him to have picked up on this colloquialism. How perceptive! How socially astute! Perhaps I needed to work on my communication skills! Now, whenever I preface speaking with the unnecessary 'so,' I think of Ross and enjoy a great laugh.

Ross and his family have taught me so much. One particular heart-to-heart that I had with Linda has stuck with me. I don't remember how we got to talking about this, but Linda explained she would never want Ross to not have autism. She talked about the ways autism makes him who he is and that if she could wave a magic wand she would never take the autism away. Teary-eyed, I listened and agreed wholeheartedly with her. Why would anyone want him to be any different? He brings color to the black and white personalities out there and for this we're most gifted and most thankful.

That said, I have often thought of how challenging raising Ross must be and how frustrating the symptoms of autism can be, especially for as loving a mother as Linda. Ross wouldn't enter the room with the same spontaneous story that Ashley did. He'd need prompts for making conversation; he'd offer stiff hugs. In doing the behavior modification work, Linda and I often talked about strategies and suggestions being like double-edged swords. In trying to help Ross, sometimes we were "damned if we did and damned if we didn't." Sometimes we didn't know what to do in the moment or what should be done in the future. During these uncertain times we continued with what we knew and with what was working. We continued to show Ross love. We brought him into the treatment and learned from him. We gave things time. And, along the way, all of us utilized a lot of hugs and a lot of humor. In the colorful world of autism, you just have to. To acquaint you with the amazing author you are about to get to know, and in closing, I'd like to share this poem I wrote about her years ago...

She glides through life gracefully,
Warmth radiating from her being.
It's in her eyes, her gestures, her
Spirit
Reaching out to greet you –
Meeting heart to heart.
Not one would guess
her day to day dance
with double-edged swords –
for she finds her smile
all the while...

Jenn Reges, LICSW

Beating the Odds at Autism

Chapter 1

———◆———

Highlights of My Life

I am writing this on a flight back from Europe (listening to John Coltrane) after spending 10 days with my husband on the Western Mediterranean... visiting picturesque villages on the French Riviera, the romantic towns of Italy and the beauty of Spain. We celebrated our 25th Wedding Anniversary this year in spite of the fact that 80% of marriages having a child with autism don't survive.

If someone were to ask what our "secret" is, I would say it's as simple as this: Don't lose yourself in the syndrome. Yes, you are a parent of a child with autism...okay...enough said. However, you are also your spouse's partner, lover and perhaps a parent to other children, as well. You are also a daughter, maybe a sister or aunt, friend, neighbor and perhaps student, employee or professional. You need to remember that if you are to have balance in your life, you can't do it alone. If you try to, you will be sacrificing in other areas that make you complete. You will then create an environment where your spouse and other children will begin to feel neglected, or perhaps even bitter.

I remember quite a few years back, when Ashley came downstairs on a school day to have breakfast, I was in the kitchen where I always waited for her and Ross. When I greeted her with a "good morning kiss," she gave me a smile and I said, "What's the matter?" She responded, "Mom, you greet Ross and me every morning as if you haven't seen us for a week and we just said goodnight a few hours ago." I thought to myself, that's probably because I've had a chance to "recharge" since thankfully I sleep so soundly! I then thought to myself, well, I hope I continue to greet you two and those I care about that way, because it will be a sign that I'm managing this balancing act we call life!

So my advice to you is this, if someone offers to watch your child and you feel they're capable, say yes. If the child study team recommends full days of preschool versus half days, agree to it. If you have the luxury of family or friends offering an overnight stay to your child, don't deny yourself that. Time away is time to recharge and this is vital if you are going to meet and exceed your child's needs and his or her expectations of you (see later chapter entitled Living in the Moment.) This opening chapter may seem like an odd place to begin writing a book about growing up with autism; however, as you read on, I think you'll see the importance of not letting autism consume you and it will make sense why I'm reaching out to parents in my opening chapter.

I oftentimes listened to friends, family and neighbors' worries about their son or daughter not making the travel soccer team or not getting the lead in the school play, and thought to myself, everything really is relative in life. You really do need to put everything into perspective. And while at times, these milestones may be very important to a child as well as a parent, and rightly so, it's the milestones of a child with autism that create a different sense of satisfaction and pride. Having my son Ross and daughter Ashley has taught me to revel in all the milestones, just at different phases and at different levels. It's not to say I was any less excited over Ashley's achievements and successes, it's just to say that Ross' struggles and challenges were different and brought about a different sense of accomplishment as a parent. If I can put it simply, sharing in Ross' accomplishments has made me more "available" to Ashley's disappointments. In other words, it's feeling that you can be perfectly happy with imperfect outcomes!

You see, while children learn from their environment, children with autism do not. So you painstakingly have to teach every self-help skill, the basic manners, and appropriate behavior in certain situations. And you're teaching these self-help skills to a child with fine and gross motor skills deficits, who is not always cooperative...if you get the idea! Now, parents may say, well, we've had to teach those things to our children as well and they're not autistic. Agreed. However, your children also "picked up" the social cues and appropriate behaviors from others. When you compound the fact that autism has been described by many as being similar to visiting a foreign country and not speaking the language, you can imagine how difficult it is to potty train or teach appropriate eating techniques or something as mundane as teeth brushing when they're "not getting" the everyday nuances of life.

Autistic two-year-olds bring new meaning to the phrase "Terrible Twos"!!! I can reflect back to a visit to the supermarket when Ross was tantruming in the shopping cart. (I might add, reading the signs all the while at age 2: Delicatessen, Pharmacy – blowing my mind!) The "easy" thing to do would have been to give in and give him the chips or whatever he was screaming for; the difficult thing was pulling the cart to the side of the aisle, my daughter Ashley by my side all the while, and waiting until he stopped and behaved appropriately by "asking nicely" so as not to reinforce his inappropriate behavior. This would only lead to more tantrums and meltdowns when he failed to get something he wanted in the future. So as those peering eyes would pass, as mothers looked down their nose at me, one mother did have the audacity to ask: Wow, a little spoiled; isn't he? Can't you control the outbursts in public? So as my eyes welled up with tears, I simply replied: He's just having a bad day. I then looked at Ross (and Ashley who was so in tune with the situation and my response) and thought to myself: If she only knew...

So back to the beginning of this chapter. The mere fact that we are able to go to Europe and leave our children with my parents is a blessing. We've worked tirelessly since Ross was young to instill independence and self-help skills. I think it speaks volumes that we were able to chance taking an extended vacation, especially since he is only a sophomore in high school at the time of this writing. A significant reason that we were able to even entertain the thought...after all, we're talking Europe versus vacationing within the US...is due to his older sister Ashley who is a senior in high school at this time. Ashley has always been a little mother to Ross, in addition to being a sister, friend, teacher, therapist, mentor and role model. Ashley wore and continues to wear many hats. We just knew in our hearts that with us gone, Ashley would be able to keep things in order and guide my parents in any questions they had when it came to Ross. At times during the past 16 years, I have actually felt that Ashley could just step in and take over if something were to happen to me.

So, needless to say, here we are on our way back from Barcelona and it was business as usual while we were gone. No one skipped a beat and Ross was able to attend every tutoring session, football practice, bowling tryouts, etc. Life is good!

Now, if you were to ask me what the highlights of my trip were, I could easily recite something about each country and towns in which I have unfinished business and NEED to return to. If you were to ask me what the highlight of my time away was, it would be this. While speaking to Ross from Italy, seven days into the trip, I asked him if he missed me (an emotion that is difficult for these kids to experience, let alone express.) His response was this, "I miss you, Mom, but I just want you to have a good time since you deserve it." Now, while this was somewhat of a patterned or scripted response, I truly feel it was genuine. Things have been placed into such perspective for me that this comment stirred the same joy that being in Europe did, because it was another milestone - - not only in our marriage and celebrating that special anniversary in Europe - - but a milestone in our son's development, and that's something money can't buy.

When you stumble across these milestones that have not or could not be "taught", it's incredible. It's a feeling that surpasses any other "tangible" goal (i.e., potty training, phrasing, fine/gross motor skills, riding a bicycle.) From the initial diagnosis, these feelings have always been and will continue to be highlights for me!

Highlights of My Life

Beating the Odds at Autism

Chapter 2

---◆---

The Jackpot Diagnosis

I'm still on the flight back from Spain - - now listening to Miles Davis - - and decide to get another chapter done. As you might have guessed by now, I'm quite the jazz aficionado! Jazz is a lot like autism...very interpretive and, at times, tells a story without words.

While not wanting to get too deep into "the history of Ross" some readers may find it helpful to know that Ross did not receive his diagnosis of Autism/PDD-NOS until the ripe old age of three-and-a-half. As we know now, this is very late in the game, as half of what we know we learn by the age of five. At the time of this writing, November of '07, legislation has just been passed that will mandate that physicians screen for signs of autism twice by a child's 18-month checkup. This is riveting and should be so encouraging for parents, and for this reason. While you are seeing "signs" and suspecting that "something just isn't right" from early on, you'll have family members and friends, perhaps even your child's pediatrician and maybe even your spouse, tell you to just wait and see. Now parents won't have to wait and see. Your pediatrician will be your guide and you collaboratively can begin the process of identifying if your child needs to begin a course of evaluations to receive his or her diagnosis.

You are, of course, never relieved to get the diagnosis since there is no cure. However, your child has a better chance at a fulfilling life if early intervention was to begin at 18 months or earlier versus three-and-a-half years. We had a lot of catching up to do in a small window of time. There may be gaps in Ross' language development that we will never be able to bridge; nonetheless, these gaps usually go unnoticed since he's so masterful at overcompensating for them.

The benefit of having your pediatrician perform screenings on your pre-18-month-old will remove the guessing game for you and your family. In my case, at the time I was working full time for Bell Atlantic in Philadelphia. I knew that Ross was in ways a bit different than his two-year-older sister Ashley had been at his age. It wasn't just the lack of spontaneous language...at the time he had perhaps a 50-word vocabulary but wasn't phrasing...it was more the fact that he was a space cadet. I could ask him his name or if he wanted pancakes for breakfast, and he'd look at me like I was a million miles away. However, he could be in another room and if I asked him if he wanted to watch Sesame Street, he'd come running. It was, yes, selective; but yet erratic in ways I can't explain. I just knew that something wasn't right and it was time to find out what that "something" was. I chose to take one of the buyouts from Bell Atlantic and decided to give Ross the extra time he needed at home with me one-on-one.

The first thing I did was to go to our EIRC (Educational Instructional Resource Center) in our Township which proved to be a Godsend. I applied for a membership and would go weekly and checkout teachers' tools for teaching preschoolers. I then chose to go back to school and enrolled in classes three nights a week year-round. I would work with Ross during the day and leave tasks and exercises for my husband to work on at night with him while I was at school. The results were hard to measure and we could see no concrete improvement, but after all, we weren't teaching professionals. We were parents trying to achieve some sort of result; some sort of response; some sort of stimulation.

Of course, this was 1992, pre the resources that the internet now avails us to. So I went to the library and took out every book I could on developmental delays, including autism. Well, this took away all of the guessing on my part. I remember coming home one night after class, 10:30 p.m., and having at least five books opened on the kitchen table and crying. Ross was autistic. I immediately called my pediatrician's service, had him paged and he called me back immediately. When he asked: Who's sick, Ross or Ashley? I replied: Ross is autistic. He calmly asked me why I believed this, and I went on to reiterate excerpts from each book and how they related to Ross...tears dripping onto the textbooks the entire time. He then calmly said: You know, in my many years of practice, I've only had one other child with autism and Ross is nothing like that child. However, when a Mother tells me something's wrong, I trust the Mother. Let's get the ball rolling. Let's start with his hearing,

---

The Jackpot of Diagnosis

perhaps it's his hearing. We'll then move on to a developmental screening. I adamantly knew it wasn't his hearing. Not only had Ross never had an ear infection, his hearing was overly acute at times that he could hear me from another room. I also knew that it would be difficult to convince a panel of doctors that Ross was autistic, because he did display some eye contact, was warm and cuddly at times, and had many strengths. But I was ready to get the ball rolling and prepared myself for the diagnosis of autism.

Our first visit found us at the office of an otolaryngologist. Ross was very compliant during the hearing evaluation and, as I had suspected, his hearing tested fine. While that would be of some comfort to other parents, it was the evidence I needed to confirm that my gut feeling was correct and I was leaning towards a developmental delay...at this point I was keeping all bets open, but my money was on autism.

We then visited with a developmental specialist. At this visit, Ross was observed by a panel of professionals: developmental, speech and psychology. I remember sitting there, nervously observing and not quite knowing what to wish for. Do I want Ross to complete the tasks in a timely, acceptable fashion and have him go undiagnosed, or misdiagnosed; or do I want him to exhibit his true self, which I see at home, and receive the diagnosis of autism? You know, it's a perplexing thing. You listen to family and friends who caringly suggest, maybe you're being too hard on him; maybe he'll catch up in time; and even going so far as, maybe you're comparing him to Ashley and you want a perfect little boy and you shouldn't compare siblings, let alone, male and female. But then, when you are in a bakery and he is handed a cookie and doesn't look or acknowledge the person and, of course, doesn't say thank you because he isn't speaking, you hear, "You have to start teaching him manners." My prayer to God at this point was to give me the strength to accept the diagnosis - - not to change it - - and for the wisdom and guidance which I would need because it was not an area that I was familiar or comfortable with as a parent or professional.

So, now, off we went to Jefferson Hospital in Philadelphia to see a highly-regarded pediatric neurologist. I remember walking from the parking lot in Center City Philadelphia, the hustle and bustle of workday traffic, and feeling like we were the only three on the street. I was just oblivious to my surroundings. Now that I think about it, probably mimicking the way Ross goes through his day. I'll never forget being in the waiting room and asking for the strength to be strong for my husband if the words came out of the physician's mouth, "Yes, Mr. and Mrs. Burns, your son has autism." I thought about how my husband would react to the words, since up until this point he had been in denial. I wondered how my husband, who grew up playing ice hockey and was an all-around sports enthusiast, would handle hearing the words about his son...his boy...his future ice hockey player. I guess I would soon find out, because I just knew it was an impending diagnosis which we would receive today.

The doctor came out, shook our hands and introduced himself. He then, in a very matter-of-fact fashion, put Ross through a series of tasks in which he observed and took copious notes. After about an hour, he looked across his desk at us and said, "Yes, Mr. and Mrs. Burns, your son has autism." In all of my reading and research, the one thing that stuck in my mind is that autism is a spectrum disorder, and that was a glimmer of hope for me. In my attempts to be strong, I asked, "How severe do you think he is"? He said, I would suggest enrolling him in a preschool program for children with special needs and teach him Sign Language (ASL) because he'll <u>never develop any useful language.</u> Now, I do not want you parents who are reading this to be discouraged. We never taught Ross Sign Language except for the little bit that he learned in the preschool program initially. The special education teachers, speech pathologists and occupational therapists there were very in tune with Ross. And they agreed to allow him to Sign in an effort to elicit language but not have him Sign as a crutch, but rather as a temporary tool. Although his language is labored at times, he is fluent and quite skilled in his use of the English language (as you'll experience firsthand later in this book as he shares his thoughts and advice) along with being fluent in Spanish, I might add! Just don't take what anyone tells you as the end-all. Our kids continually amaze us and please, please, please...don't ever show them that you're discouraged.

My husband then asked the neurologist how Ross differed from other children that he's diagnosed with autism. The physician casually said that although autism is usually coupled with mental retardation, he didn't believe this was the case with Ross; however, we would, of course, be undergoing further testing. I turned and looked at my husband in an attempt to follow this response up with something, but I just couldn't find the right words at the time.

I remember leaving Jefferson Hospital in Philadelphia and walking back to the parking garage...my husband and I both had Ross by the hands, swinging him over the curbs while waiting for the red lights to turn, and not speaking at all to each other. What was there to say? I, at least, wasn't surprised by the diagnosis; however, my husband was crushed by the diagnosis. He was "holding out hope" and was anxiously waiting to prove me wrong...which I would have loved to have heard the words from him "I told you so" in this instance. So now we would either join a support group for parents of autistic children where we would commiserate and say, "Why us; why Ross?" or, we could now put on our game face and research every conventional and unconventional treatment, therapy, intervention and modality out there and guide our son to a happy, productive, independent life...the latter was our choice.

I first set out to visit schools in New Jersey for autistic children. I realize that some parents reading this may beg to differ, but we felt so fortunate to be here due to the fact that New Jersey and Delaware are the two most progressive states when it comes to autism education and intervention. My experience... and not being a political person, I might add...is that New Jersey has really made the diagnosis and treatment of autism spectrum disorders a top priority. And as for our School District of Washington Township, we've had families relocate here from as far away as Hawaii because of our reputation. From our first meeting with the Child Study Team when Ross was three-and-a-half we have had nothing but cooperation and support from the District and that is something I will be forever thankful for. After visiting several nationally-recognized schools, I just felt that that placement was not right for Ross.

We then enrolled Ross in the preschool program for special needs children in our Township. I also researched Applied Behavioral Analysis (ABA) therapy which I found to be the most effective, evidence-based treatment for children with autism. My husband and I then presented it to our School District who embraced the idea and said, "We've never done it before. We heard that it started out at UCLA. Educate us; tell us what you need us to do; and we'll get the ball rolling." What else can a parent ask for; we had their support.

So in collaboration with the School District, we began interviewing prospective ABA therapists. Once we had our "team" we selected a consultant who came highly recommended and held a two-day workshop at our home for therapists and family members. Ross then began undergoing 40 hours of ABA, 10 of which my husband and I would do, which would take place seven days a week. This was the beginning of "walking the walk and talking the talk." I will never forget the commitment and dedication of these therapists. They would start out working, perhaps, four hours a week and then once – as they affectionately termed it – they "caught the Ross thing" they would increase the number of hours they'd commit to. This "Ross thing" was infectious and these therapists became part of our family. They would spend holidays with us, at times we would bring them along on vacations, and we have shared in their courtships, marriages and births of their children. In a way we adopted them...but thank goodness we didn't have to pay for their college tuition!

Ross was attending the preschool program in the Washington Township School District on Monday through Thursday mornings where he received occupational and speech therapy daily. The second year of preschool, we moved him to a typical preschool in the Township, accompanied by one of his ABA therapists who functioned as a shadow (a shadow aids the teacher when it comes to Ross without providing hand-over-hand instruction) in the preschool class. This continued until

Ross attended Kindergarten where he also had a shadow. He then decreased his hours to 30 hours a week since Kindergarten was five mornings a week. He kept up this pace of 30 hours a week well into middle school, at which time his weekly hours would be reduced according to his mastery of the skills we were teaching. These skills would encompass anything from self-help skills, to gross/fine motor skills, decoding, etc. Imagine finding 30 "extra" hours in your week to be committed to something, 12 months a year, year in and year out, and never really being given an opportunity to complain. It's no wonder that Ross takes nothing for granted.

An interesting point to bring out about Ross is this...he never wanted to be treated differently. And in respecting that, we put the same social and behavioral demands on Ross as we did on Ashley. And along with those demands came consequences (which at times would crush us to impose.) However, we knew one of our goals was to raise a little boy who would not only know the difference between right and wrong, but would be responsible for his actions and learn from his mistakes. All the while we were role modeling and teaching respect, not only for others, but self-respect (and we prayed that society would respect Ross and his differences at the same time.) In looking back, I feel that this probably helped Ashley to see that her brother didn't receive preferential treatment because he learned differently. He was consequenced for the same things that she would be consequenced for. I remember hoping at the time that by doing so, we would allay any resentment that Ashley could have felt had we allowed him to get away with things that she could not. Some behaviors are learned and, in my eyes, can be shaped. Other behaviors at times are symptoms of the disorder and can at least be minimized to the point of social acceptability and I would suspect, as in the case of others, be significantly improved by the use of medication.

Ross is 16 at the writing of this chapter and is on no medications other than a multi-vitamin. We did a two-week blind trial of Adderall in fourth grade in an attempt to improve his focus; it was not a good fit for Ross. Although he was the first to complete his quizzes in class, the Adderall increased his obsessive compulsive behaviors significantly, which he also exhibits. Also, when he was coming off the meds at nighttime, he became so agitated that he didn't seem like the same Ross. Although I don't want to suggest that meds aren't helpful in some children with autism, I just feel that we Americans have a pill to fix everything, albeit sometimes a quick fix. I also realize that there are sometimes overlapping diagnoses which mandate the need for medication. With Ross' level of the disorder, we chose to take the sometimes-more-difficult approach and attempt to fix/minimize/improve the target behavior without the use of medication which can sometimes "mask" the behavior, even though the neurologist wrote the script for an anti-anxiety medication and said to give it a try. (I elaborate on the medication decision in Chapter 3.) I truly would never withhold anything that would enable Ross to be more comfortable in our world. I like the fact that in a few years he will be able to make that decision for himself...

(At the end of freshman year, Ross was having difficulty with final exam preparation and said it was just really hard to focus. I asked Ross if he wanted to give the Adderall or perhaps some other drug another try and he said, "No thanks, I'll just have to try harder.")

So the end result is, Ross may require a little extra time to accomplish a task, or he may ask you to repeat something and say he didn't hear you – all the while he did, he's just stalling for time to comprehend – he is okay with that and so are we.

Beating the Odds at Autism

Chapter 3

---◆---

Back at the Beach

Well, it's been a year since I wrote the Preface of this book on the beach, and Ross has grown in so many ways during that time. At the time the kids and I decided to write this book, we decided to not put any deadline on it or ourselves, since we had so much more life to live and experience which would only provide more valuable information for us to pass on...so here we are a year later! Before I share one significant component to Ross' ability to deal with stress, I want to share an exchange I had on the beach today.

When I parked my chair in the sand at 10 a.m. it was literally just "me and the seagulls." I thought to myself initially, wow, this will be a great day to work on the beach. There will be no distractions, not even the occasional jogger or fisherman to draw my attention. It will be a day of just the brilliant sun against a background of blue. But then after taking another glimpse around, I immediately called my husband to find out if perhaps the beach was closed for some environmental reason...because I'm the only one here! He assured me that it's safe to be there as he heard nothing to the contrary in the news and reminded me that it is mid-week and people do work and it's only April in New Jersey! So here I sit. I decided I would segment my day and work on proofreading transcripts (I am a freelance court reporter) on my laptop from 10-12 and then move on to my leisure reading and journaling! While deep into my editing...and I won't dare mention which one of my attorney clients' case I'm working on because I know in advance you'll all buy my book!...I hear a voice coming from the rear.

"You know, I was hoping the beach would be empty today and now I'm afraid we're going to have trouble finding a spot!" Well, I turned, made eye contact with an attractive mid-60ish couple and broke into laughter. I said, "You're the first sign of human life I've seen since 10 a.m., I really hope you two can keep the noise down!" They laughed and, just as wittingly as this gentleman made that intro, we began to engage in an inquisitive, but very natural exchange. They shared that they were retired; I shared I was jealous. I said that I was working; he said, you could have fooled me. He asked what I did; I told him I was a court reporter. He said their son went to school for court reporting but dropped out; I said, smart man! He asked how long I'd been doing it; I said that I left my job at Bell Atlantic and entered school when my son was diagnosed with autism. He said, wow, you chose the second most stressful profession next to air traffic controllers; I said, well, stress is relative when you have a child with autism.

After our ten or fifteen minutes of banter, we wished each other well and I sat and thought about why we were able to make this connection. We both gave something to each other and that's what I marveled at and was having fun pondering. I then got thinking about how selfish it was of me to make that final comment about stress and relating it to having a child with autism. My thoughts moved to...everything is, in fact, relative. My stress level can't compare in the least to the stress that Ross has felt over the years trying to fit into our perfect little world.

Anxiety, aggression and attention are all areas that are affected by sensory overload issues. I think back to about five years ago when Ross was in the fourth grade, struggling with anxiety and the social demands of friends and students who were once accepting of Ross' idiosyncrasies, who have now become mocking and cruel. I'm sure you parents have heard this a thousand times, "Kids will be kids." But as I'm sure many of you know, when it's your kid, there's nothing worse. So we found ourselves in the neurologist's office asking for advice. The doctor was very readily willing to hand me a script for Zoloft. I graciously took it and said I would tuck it away. He also said this to me: Mrs. Burns, I have to tell you that if Ross were my son, knowing what I know, I would have traced your exact steps. You're now hitting a roadblock, but there's still time for meds if you choose to take that path in the future. (This is in no way meant to offend anyone who is on Zoloft or any of the SSRIs, which are so beneficial to so many.) I just feel that here in America we are so apt to pop a pill for everything, versus the Europeans, and it appeared as though I had found a pediatric neurologist who felt the same way I did. I left there with Ross and thought to myself, "I vow that I will never withhold anything from Ross that will make him more comfortable in "our world." But for now, it just doesn't feel right...

I researched a therapist with the appropriate training in sensory integration therapy from Australia. This Australian occupational therapist was working in a hospital outpatient facility; she came highly recommended, highly priced (not covered by insurance), and she shared my views on medication. I needed to become educated regarding how sensory processing problems can influence children on the spectrum. I immediately felt that I had come to the right place. After completing mountains of paperwork, she totally understood the issues that Ross faced throughout his day even before attempting to meet with him. She was very confident that she could help minimize his heightened reactions and was eager to get started by seeing him three times a week for eight weeks straight. She would set out to devise a sensory diet, if you will, consisting of alerting, organizing and calming activities which would meet the needs of Ross' nervous system specifically. Knowledge is empowerment, and I finally felt that someone else "got it" and we were on our way to helping Ross with some coping mechanisms.

Sensory integration therapy focuses primarily on three basic senses; tactile, vestibular and proprioceptive. Many of our kids' behaviors, which I believe are symptoms of the disorder, manifest themselves in the tactile (touch) system, especially overreacting to seemingly harmless sensory experiences. Ross would only wear "smooth" clothing and eat "smooth" foods (and this wasn't as simple as cutting the tags out of his clothing.) Although he loved yogurt at a young age, shame on you if you bought the "fruit on the bottom" as you'd immediately send him into a display of gagging. He was also extremely sensitive to light touch which made showering, haircuts and getting caught in the rain unbearable. Theoretically, overstimulation of the brain is caused by the tactile system not functioning properly and therefore sending "whacky" neural signals. These "whacky" neural signals lead to these "whacky" (negative) emotional responses to touch. (How scientifically-astute are my adjectives!)

What I'm attempting to convey above to parents, teachers and caregivers is this...there is a problem with modulation, i.e., turning up or down the volume on a sensory input that comes into the brain. The brain then can't modulate the information it gets and it can then go into overload, and the result can be inappropriate behavior or withdrawal in the case of a defensive response. So it's not so much "whacky signals" as it is the brain's inability to handle what it receives from the body and environment. The signals are okay; it's the brain's inability to interpret them that's the problem.

As you may be aware, the vestibular system, referring to the inner ear, accounts for the "whacky" behaviors, such as; spinning, jumping and twirling when in dysfunction. And then the proprioceptive system applies to our muscles, joints and tendons. This system allows us to master our fine motor skills as well as praxis and motor planning. Dysfunction in this arena accounts for the clumsiness and lack of awareness of body positioning, i.e., personal space. We had to model appropriate personal space to Ross at a young age because he thought he had to be right up on top of another child in order to get their attention. It's estimated that 2 million bits per second enter the central nervous system. I don't know about you but that's enough proof that we need to regulate it if we can, not only in children with autism but in all of us.

I must say to parents that "this was the biggest bang for our buck." Not only was Ross receptive to the therapist's strategies for proactively preparing for stressful situations and coping once in a stressful situation, he was excited about putting her strategies to work and "feeling" (pardon the pun!) the benefits. This not only helped quell Ross' anxiety issues, but also the challenges he had with overstimulation, sensory concerns and tactile defensiveness. When you think about it, the nervous system is remarkable; that is, when it's not in overload. Think about how many times throughout the course of a typical day we need to regulate ours. It's not rocket science (forgive me, Jenny...I respect what you do!) it's just creating the awareness and forethought to be proactive to avoid meltdowns. And who amongst us doesn't know at least one individual who doesn't have autism who wouldn't benefit by avoiding meltdowns!

Perhaps better said...it's the intervention that is simple, i.e., not rocket science; it all makes sense. However, the interpretation of theory and what might be going on does take advanced knowledge by a trained professional and we had "hit the jackpot" when we connected with Jenny!

Ashley became an altar server at our church in 3rd grade and Ross followed suit. They were on the same "altar server" team so it was a beautiful thing. Ashley was there to guide and Ross was thrilled to be up on the altar, as he takes his religion very seriously. I find it amazing, though, that Ross is one of the most open-minded teenagers I know when it comes to learning about other religions and being accepting. While this all sounds so good, it was so disturbing to be in the first pew, proud as any parent would be, and watch Ross transform during certain parts of the Mass that were over-stimulating to him; i.e., ringing of the bells, the choir singing, the organ, the acoustics, the congregation reciting prayers. I actually found myself angry with God at times while I watched. I would pray...(okay, maybe yell)..."he's in your house trying to serve you and you can't help him control his anxiety and self-stimulatory behaviors!!!" (Lesson here...I always made up with The Man upstairs!!!) Ross would exhibit signs of overstimulation by putting his hands up to his ears, rocking, grimacing...which any of the three would remove his focus and make Ashley's job much harder on the altar.

Now, we could have filled that script for Zoloft (or some other antianxiety med) and perhaps he would have been more relaxed, but we chose to teach him strategies, with the guidance of our occupational therapist skilled in sensory integration, which will prove to be lifelong tools in any anxiety-producing situation. These strategies ranged from working out beforehand, chewing gum, sucking on a mint or lemon drop, deep pressure with a brush (which is actually deep pressure followed by proprioception that has to do with the nervous system as a whole) and many other modalities too many to mention. Ross was also diagnosed with migraines in the fourth grade, which these sensory modalities certainly played a role in minimizing, along with teaching the importance of hydration, timely meals and "being aware" of the aura in an effort to get a jump on Ibuprofen. Ross was eventually able to "feel" the signs his body was sending and this helped him modulate what was to follow.

I thoroughly believe that when a child is diagnosed with autism, the path should include: speech therapy and OT with an occupational therapist who has postgraduate training in sensory integration techniques. It came to the point where the sensory issues were starting to overshadow the stereotypical issues of autism.

At the time of this writing, occupational therapy with an OT trained in sensory integration is not covered by insurance, as not enough research has been done regarding the benefits. I had gone before the Board of our insurance company, accompanied by my pediatrician, to "present our case." We had 20 minutes to convince a team of doctors, psychologists, psychiatrists and lawyers that they should reconsider coverage for OT with sensory integration training. My pediatrician and I were accompanied to the elevators after our presentation and congratulated. It was also brought to my attention that a pediatrician had never accompanied a parent before the Board as my pediatrician did...and this spoke volumes in my eyes of our relationship and his fondness for Ross. We left feeling hopeful, only to learn four weeks later that regrettably there would be no coverage for this $300/hour-three-times-a-week therapy that was so vital to our son...

Note: I am thrilled to report that midway through the publication of this book, in August of 2009, Governor Jon S. Corzine enacted legislation that, for the very first time, mandates that New Jersey health insurers provide coverage for screening of autism and other developmental delays. The legislation, S1650/A2238, requires insurance companies to provide coverage of evidence-based, medically necessary autism therapies - a staggering $36,000 annually for a child with autism who is 21 years of age or younger. Some of the evidence-based behavioral interventions include occupational, physical and speech therapy...these driving therapies that can change the path for your child and undeniably allow them to reach the goals that we all have as parents. And let's face it, at the time of this publication, many families are being stretched thin financially, not just New Jersey residents. However, it's quite easy...trust me...for families of children with autism to bankrupt themselves in order to provide some of these therapies; such as, ABA, in order to feel that they've given their child the best opportunity for a full life, and now this law will better position them. And although the timing of our family situation did not afford us the benefit, I am so thankful that other families won't have to make the never-ending sacrifices that we did to gain the same favorable results. In my opinion, there's no time like the present to avail your child to every therapeutic intervention out there. My approach was always this...I'd rather do more than find out I missed the window of opportunity and didn't do enough.

Let's hear how Ross felt about the benefits of sensory therapy:

When I was very young, not too much of the sensory therapy helped me out because I wasn't old enough to understand how parts of sensory therapy could help me release the stress. When I was in fourth or fifth grade, my mom always helped me with exercising; such as, lifting weights, wearing the ankle weights while walking around, and everything else that was hard for me to do, which is now easy since I've been lifting weights throughout high school with the football team. All I did when I was younger as far as a workout was just sitting on a bouncy ball moving up and down and all around, but I still had stress. And that is why a year or two later, I was a little bit chubby since I wasn't getting enough exercise.

But it's all behind me now that I am very healthy, less stressed, and well-focused in school and will be later in college as well. I'll just figure out things that I can do to keep on releasing all the stress as I get older. Like, if I decide to become a blackjack dealer in the casino (hopefully the Borgata!) and customers start to go crazy on me. My mom reminds me that I won't be able to "react" if a customer at my table loses and starts to yell at me, or if a customer gives me a hard time. I'll have to put the strategies that I learned into use in those situations or else I'll get fired.

I've been getting less stressed as I've been maturing year after year, compared to what was happening during my earlier childhood, like while I was in elementary school. Yet, I found that in middle school I had about 50 percent of stress, but I still worked things out to get prepared for high school. Eighth grade was one of my greatest memories from middle school. Now that I'm in high school there was more stress I've expunged by getting busier with my school work, especially studying and preparing to pass quizzes and tests, and playing football and golf for Washington Township High School. However, when I struggle in some subjects that I take, some of the stress comes back to me and I react the same way as I did throughout elementary and middle school. But I've been thinking positive and fixing my mistakes, as I always do, and I want to continue to do that, especially while in the work world.

I thought positive when I retook the English section of the HSPA in October and what happened when I found out my results two months later...I had finally passed and I had a score of 207 and my English teacher was so proud of me for my effort. This is how I should be when I'm in college and possibly dealer school...always think and be positive, whether you succeed from the beginning or make some mistakes along the way.

And this advice always should go to the Phillies, Eagles, Flyers, and Sixers, that way they will succeed while still releasing the stress! Go Philadelphia Teams!!!

It appears as though Ross is happy and engaged while on the school playground...he is really engrossed in self-stimulatory behavior.

Chapter 4

---◆---

If Only You Could Feel
What I Feel

Ashley will be leaving for college in a few weeks. It's been quite exciting the last few months between visiting colleges, her senior trip to Florida, prom, graduation ceremonies, parties, and commencement. I thought often about how Ross might be handling all of this. For a change, the focus was off of him and on Ashley.

From the time Ross was diagnosed, one of my fears was that I would unintentionally "push Ashley aside" because she was always such an easy kid who required very little. And as much as I hate to admit it, the reality was I could see that happening in the throes of Ross' early intervention. After all, Ross attended the preschool program 15 hours a week (three hours a day; Monday through Friday) and then did 40 hours of ABA therapy per week (this was spread out over seven days a week.) This was eventually decreased to 30 hours a week once

---

Ross was in school for five full days a week. Initially, ten of the 40 hours of ABA, my husband and I did with him. Our becoming involved in the therapy was designed so that we never turned off ABA; we learned to walk the walk and talk the talk.

So needless to say, our house was like a revolving door seven days a week in order to fit these sessions in. And, yes, everyone who came and went through that revolving door was there for Ross; thus my concern that Ashley might grow up with a little bit of resentment. Therefore, I told the tutors/therapists from the very beginning that if they ever saw me unintentionally pushing Ashley aside, to just be forthright and tell me (and then slap me!)

I'd be remiss if I didn't add what a vital part Ashley played in Ross' development. What better way to teach reciprocal play, turn-taking and sharing than with a typical kid! It's something that just wouldn't have had the same impact on Ross had it been modeled by the tutors or myself. And what a good role model Ashley was...and a natural at ABA, I might add. Ross and Ashley shared friends who were siblings...(and those of you reading this know who you are!)...and that was a beautiful thing when it came to sleepovers, birthday parties and the like. It was so positive and so beneficial and so perfect to have another set of siblings to model everything that we wanted to teach to Ross.

I will never be able to express my appreciation to those friends of ours who played such an important part in Ross' childhood. I can only imagine how difficult it was opening their home to Ross and not feeling completely comfortable that they knew what to do, or what not to do, during one of his temper tantrums or meltdowns, or simply when he was not able to express himself and his needs. But they, and we, felt somewhat at ease as long as Ashley was there. Our friends would comment on how she would just simply stop doing what she was doing and "step in" when they looked to her for guidance. Because of the willingness and kindness of our friends and family, we were able to create memories in every activity from Boy Scouts to Christmas Caroling to trips to the beach...and that certainly contributed to a happy childhood for Ross and Ashley in the midst of our unconventional family dynamics!!!

(Now back to my thoughts three paragraphs ago about Ashley growing up with resentment. I apologize. I'm having some focusing issues here!)

Well, as far as growing up somewhat resentful, that might have happened to another kid, but not Ashley. She rose to every challenge and became a big sister, tutor, therapist, friend, role model, peer role model, and advocate, even at the ripe old age of six or seven! As she matured into early teens, she also became a confidant and therapist for her mother, as well. She was, and is, always there to bounce ideas off of and I value her advice and wisdom. The amazing thing about Ashley is, we read each other and she'll sense that I need someone to talk to before I even broach the subject. She has an innate quality that will make her an asset to the world of psychology and many clients will benefit from her experience and "worldly wisdom" as I like to call it, all the while never having to leave our home! She's gotten a real education!

I'd like to share a little secret. As I'm writing this, her father doesn't know it, but Ross and I do. Ashley came to me...even though she's 18 at the time of this writing and

---

If Only You Could Feel What I Feel

doesn't require my permission...and said she wanted to get a tattoo in an inconspicuous spot to signify her relationship with Ross. I asked her what it was and she told me a "mommy" bird with her "baby" flying below to forever remind her of how she looked after Ross until he was able to "take off on his own." To this day, I will never forget that and, if only the three of us know, (well, thanks to me, her father now knows!) it is something that we will always cherish.

Ashley was just asked yesterday to speak at a workshop for siblings in the fall. I know that she will be a resource as well as an inspiration for other siblings. My only wish is that these siblings could have seen Ashley in action. Everything has always come so naturally to her. She never made a spectacle of the situation. She always sensed when she was able to back off and when she needed to move in closer while in social settings and out in public. She never wanted to stigmatize; always wanted to empower. I attribute Ross' self-confidence in social situations greatly to her ability at a young age to foster that. While I may have been viewed as an overbearing parent while at birthday parties or out in public settings, Ashley was able to discretely guide and "shadow" Ross to enable him to self-monitor and, at times, initiate interaction when appropriate. Once again, this can't be taught and can't be found in a textbook, but I'm confident that when siblings hear Ashley speak and give suggestions, they'll walk away with some useful tools to guide them in their social outings with their siblings.

All of this leads me to why I was so disappointed a few weeks ago while the four of us were out to dinner. My husband asked Ross if he was going to "miss" Ashley when she leaves for college in August. He flat out said, "No." When asked again by me (all the while I'm looking at Ashley's face drop in disbelief) he told me, pointblank, "Mom, I just can't make myself feel something like you can. I can't make myself miss her if I don't feel it."

After reflecting on this and talking to some professionals, it wasn't that Ross is uncaring or cold, it's just that it's difficult for him to project into the future and "imagine" an emotion. He has nothing to compare it to and he articulated that perfectly. I've heard over and over again that those with autism replay memories and experiences and "pull them up or recall them" when they need to in order to react, what we NT's (Neurotypicals) would view as appropriately, in certain situations. Ross had never experienced a loss up until this point and has never had the "feeling" of missing someone. So, I guess, it made sense that he honestly couldn't make himself feel that way. He had no sense of anticipation for what it might feel like.

Of course, Ashley and I have talked about this and she "gets it." She understands all too well that she has been a lifeline for Ross and he isn't yet able to express that. Perhaps we can revisit this discussion when she's gone for a while and she isn't there to drive him places or help with his homework or take him to the movies...he will certainly then have a reference point and will, perhaps, be able to "feel" the loss.

It saddens me that sometimes those living with autism get slapped with the reputation of being insensitive, shallow, and uncaring. I feel if people took the time to explore some of their reactions...or lack of reaction...that nine times out of ten there's a plausible explanation for why they may not feel what we feel. It's just that we may need to delve a little deeper and take the time to listen and try to understand.

I think you'd be interested in Ross' feelings about missing those he cares about...

I've always had different feelings and I've been maturing since I began to live in my double digits. When I was really young, I always enjoyed being with my family, including my sister, so much that I couldn't stop spending time with them. For instance, I always wanted to have sleepovers with my sister every night since I had bunk beds, so that I wouldn't have to be afraid of sleeping by myself. I'm so glad that's behind me now. After all, I will be getting my own apartment after college or I may be living on campus, depending on where I attend college.

I will still spend time with my parents, even though my sister is gone from our home by going away to college, living on campus and hanging with her friends which, of course, I like to do, too. Especially hanging out with my female friends which, of course, I think is the best!

So usually, I like to be alone, because I have busy days. Besides school, I'm involved in high school sports and other activities. I also work with my dad in his landscaping business, and that physical work along with playing sports is what makes me rest so well.

So, no, I do not sympathize with my parents about missing my sister, or missing my parents, for that matter, if I was away at college along with my sister.

When I don't see my other family relatives very often, the answer is YES! It is because I have been living with my parents and sister up until this time that my sister has gone off to college. Who I really miss are my grandparents when they're away, like on vacation. And I share my feelings with my other relatives; such as, my aunts, uncles, and cousins. Believe it or not, most teenagers are like me when it comes to these feelings about missing people, including their family members. They may just not talk honestly about it like I do.

Besides family, I'm happy that I have a bunch of friends everywhere else, besides my friends from school, and feel that I'm as popular as some other friends of mine in school. I have a bunch of contacts in my cell phone and I love to text my friends, send emails to them, and chat with them on Facebook. If I didn't have those things, I would be different than all my friends.

Sometimes I don't feel comfortable sharing feelings with my family members about who I'm going to miss or whatever. Well, it's only if I miss my mom, dad, or sister. I just don't feel it at all and it will not change, because I am a grown man for eternity...

Talking Ross through a meltdown while having a family day in New York City. It was always helpful to address situations as they would arise...and in the moment!

Chapter 5

———◆———

The Atlas of Life

I'd like to share what Ross came up with to help remain calm during the rough years of 4th and 5th grade, I'd say, at the ripe old age of 10 or so. He had been living through as many as 30-40 hours per week of ABA, spread across seven days, since he was three-and-a-half, in addition to half days initially and eventually five full days of school. Manipulation had become a problem...although we were able to diminish it and even extinguish it in certain areas with consistency amongst the therapists, tutors, teachers and family members. Consistency is the key to many therapies and interventions for autism. What happens if you're not consistent across the student's home and school environment is this...you end up "un-doing" the progress that had been made, regression sets in quickly and the student becomes resistant.

When Ross would arrive home from school, the first thing I'd do after greeting him and offering him a snack was to check his journal that his teachers completed daily of any issues that had arisen throughout the day. We literally had between 15 and 30 minutes of downtime after school before the first therapist would arrive to work with Ross for a two-hour session of ABA. The therapists would often "joke" that they were able to tell what kind of day Ross had when I greeted them at the door. They knew all-too-well that if any problematic situations took place that day, we/they would address it in his ABA session while it was fresh in his mind. This could be accomplished by simply writing a "social story" to help get the message across as to what the appropriate (desired) response or behavior should have been; or it could involve making up a mock test if there was a concept or rule that Ross was having difficulty grasping in the classroom setting.

Unfortunately, this would oftentimes cause Ross to tantrum or become oppositional and, more often than not, when the therapist would stand in my foyer before leaving for the night, the two of us would have tears in our eyes because we knew it would not be an easy "remainder of the night" coming off of a challenging session like that. And remember, after the therapist left, Ross would still have to complete homework, have dinner, bathe and manage to steal a little time for a bedtime snack and story. I get exhausted just thinking about it at my age! But it was just "part of the drill" and we just did what we had to do.

So by the 4th grade, there were still certain triggers that would cause Ross to lose privileges. Yes, that's right, Ross never had free access to TV, Nintendo, the computer...he earned his time for these activities. As militaristic as this may sound, you do not want to reward negative behavior in an autistic child. The mindset of ABA is that you are rewarded for working...not always getting the right answer...but just being available to the teaching and complying. All the while you're training the child to attend, whether it be in a mainstreamed class at school, in a social setting or an organized sport. So it had gotten to the point where he was actually "in the red" and it looked as though he would never, ever begin to earn privileges again because of his manipulation and behavior. And although a meltdown by a 10-year-old may be able to be ignored in the comfort of your own home, it is totally unacceptable in the public school setting, at a friend's house, and in public places.

We asked Ross to come up with "words" that caused him to become upset and melt down. This empowered Ross. Well, wouldn't you know it, the "words" that caused him to become upset were either commands or warnings. As innocent an exchange as a friend saying, "Watch out, Ross, a car!"...might cause Ross to lash out at the friend. So we now knew the antecedent (activity which takes place before an undesired behavior – ABC: Antecedent, Behavior; Consequence) to his lashing out, but now we needed to empower him to devise some systems to help him cope.

We asked Ross why these warnings or commands would cause him to become upset. What we were able to gather from his explanation was that he viewed this warning as his friend thinking that he wasn't smart enough to know that a car was coming, and the fact that he didn't need to be told to do something or how to do it or how to do it better. I never voiced this to any of his consultants or ABA therapists, but I suspect that this reaction came as a result of the somewhat militaristic methods of ABA therapy; wherein, the ABA therapist is somewhat of a drill sergeant. I fully understand why the

ABA therapist needs to take on that assertive role and remove the emotion from the sessions; however, I'm just mentioning this because I do believe that perhaps the method of delivery contributed to his reaction to commands as he got older.

This list was compiled and titled **The Atlas of Life** by Ross when he was 10 years old. I thought since it tied into his love of geography, it was such an appropriate, dead-on title. We had copies of it everywhere to remind him:

———◆———

Sometimes people say things that I do not like...

Directions:

Don't
No
Stop
Shhh
Hurry
Go
Wait
Turn around
Slow down

Warnings:

Be careful
Watch out
Excuse me
Pay attention
Be safe

When people say things that I do not like, I feel...

Angry
Sad
Upset
Nervous
Worried

Sometimes I become oppositional when I am nervous or upset.

When people say things that I do not like, or I feel oppositional, I need to STOP AND THINK and keep my mouth shut and then tell them "I'll be right back," and use my relaxation strategies.

Relaxation Strategies:

1. Go for a walk, if I can
2. Get a drink, if I can
3. Squeeze something in my pocket (stress ball)
4. Squeeze my hands and release my hands
5. Lift weights, if I can
6. Listen to soft music, if I can
7. Listen to my favorite music, if I can
8. Eat something, if I can
9. Say something nice
10. Sing a song, if I can
11. Say a prayer in my head
12. Say the rosary in my head
13. Say the litany in my head (Ross was very much into his religion at this time in his life and prayers were actually very calming and reinforcing for him)

The Atlas of Life

Giving Ross "13" selections to choose from always made him feel in control. He had options; he had to make a better choice; and if he did, he wouldn't be consequenced for his actions. It was a win/win. We soon observed Ross being able to control his anger more and more because we empowered him. Until today, I personally always try to include Ross in decision-making, where and when appropriate, and respect his decisions.

Think about it, do you know of a coworker or family member or friend who might benefit from the above? At least stopping and thinking before saying something they regret, right? I oftentimes think that we can all benefit from strategies to help us coexist in this very stressful world that we live in.

I'd now like for you to hear Ross' take on developing this <u>Atlas of Life</u>...

Everything I did before, like, the start of high school when all of that happened to me to get me mad was a little bit immature and careless. I would have gotten in trouble or could have ended up dead if I didn't follow instructions for safety. Now I understand all of the causes and effects around the world. I no longer need those "<u>unlucky</u>" 13 Rules or selections I can do to feel better, because I am always flexible and in control of my actions.

Like, I can pretend some things can be the same as for sports. I would not like it if I was to tell others what to do or not to do and they would get pissed off. People are trying to help others to be more safe than sorry. My mom and I can make a chapter in this book all about staying healthy and taking care of ourselves, but it's not to influence people or tell them what to do. It's just because it's the safest thing for a healthy life. There is no reason why you should deny things to help you be a perfect person, by caring about others besides yourself. Everyone knows, nobody is perfect. I would bet others did the same things as I did when younger by getting mad when you hear commands from somebody or when things don't go your way or things change without warning.

Sometimes change is good and it helps people stay flexible, not oppositional. This happens to most athletes, whether in high school, college, or the major leagues. For example, changes happen in drafts, trading players, winning or losing games, and many other things you can think of. At the time I'm writing this book, all Phillies fans were disappointed that Pat Burrell was traded to the Rays, but the good thing is we have Raul Ibanez who replaced him. That is how change is good in sports. It applies to life, as well. When things don't go our way, something unexpected can happen that would make people happier in their lives. That's why I believe that everything that happens has a purpose in life.

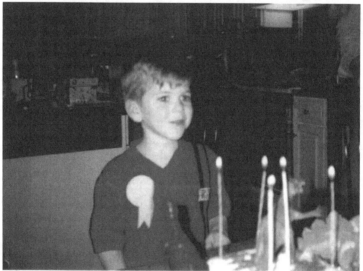

Birthdays were always difficult because of the overstimulation...always a fear of balloons popping and guests singing and clapping too loudly.

Chapter 6

Lucky 13

I always strive to find unique birthday gifts for Ashley and Ross...and turning 13 is a big milestone...and sometimes you simply can't find that perfect gift so you have to be creative!

13 Rules for Teenagers to Live By:

1. Don't repeat what actors may say that you may think is funny in a movie...they are only acting! Otherwise, others might think you're a smart aleck and have a fresh mouth.

2. Don't get into other kids' business...it will only make them dislike you.

3. Always be strong and say "no" to something you know is inappropriate to do or say.

4. Sometimes teenagers like to get teenagers in trouble, so always think before you speak or act.

5. Always make the right choice and you'll never have to worry about the consequences.

6. Always have respect for other teenagers, adults and most of all, yourself. When you have respect for yourself, you'll always want to do the right thing and be proud. You'll rarely have to be sorry for anything or have regrets.

7. Temptation is part of being a teenager...always chose right over wrong.

8. You don't have to be the most popular teenager...you only need a few good friends to be happy.

9. School is for learning; home is for flirting! Attraction and infatuation is part of life, but there is a time and place for it.

10. Always treat people the way you want to be treated and you'll never have to apologize to someone for hurting their feelings.

11. If you think something you're about to say might hurt someone's feelings, it probably will, so don't say it.

12. Teenagers should always think before they speak...sometimes it's better to just listen.

13. If you think it's hard to be a teenager, it really isn't. Just remember what a great kid you are, how you've always learned from your mistakes, and if you make the right choices as a teenager you'll mature into an adult who continues to make the right choices!

This was my "Birthday Gift" to Ross! Well, you had to see that reaction! He was mortified and said, "Do you really think my friends got a set of rules on their 13th Birthday"? I said, "No, you're the lucky one!"

For those parents of autistic children who are reading this, I don't know how it is for your child, but Ross was not able to be disciplined by using the word "no." It just caused meltdowns and manipulation. When puberty hits, it feels like a beast is being unleashed. I don't want to get into moral/religious issues here, but I am very open-minded and liberal when it comes to discussing sexuality and felt very comfortable discussing this with Ross. This is one area where I feel we can't take the "let's wait and see where it goes" approach. Since children with autism are so literal, you can imagine the consequences of not giving them a play-by-play of what their body's going through.

Once Ross really understood at this age what physical changes his body was going through and why he was feeling the way he did, he was able to grasp that he/we needed to put some systems into place to help him manage his short-temperedness before he lost every single friend and family member he had in his corner!

For those parents who haven't gone through puberty with a child with autism, I'm certain you can still relate to how challenging puberty was for, perhaps, your typically-developing child and the endless reassurance that..."this too shall pass." (That is, if we live through it!) Luckily for Ross...and more importantly us...it was short-lived. I guess those hormones had been creeping in for a while before they began racing! But nonetheless, here are some suggestions that we found helpful.

As we know, organized team sports are difficult for these kids. Even if they have the athletic ability and speed and desire, their level of alertness can be a barrier. Individualized sports (i.e., golf, tennis) were always better for Ross BUT NOT DURING PUBERTY. The lifesaver was working out with heavy weights for the calming effect. We actually worked it into his school day where he could have intermittent breaks to go down to the gym and work out with free weights and do a few pushups. He also joined the after-school weight training club which really helped him fit in while all the while doing something healthy, age-appropriate and calming. I also remember in elementary school, one of Ross' teachers even worked it into her class time, which was nice. The entire class would stand and do a few jumping jacks and pushups. We sent in a couple sets of hand weights and exercise bands and they would alternate coming to the front of the room and using them. Let's face it, it's not just kids with autism that benefit from a little mid-day aerobic exercise to get the blood flowing and help with focus and endorphins, we can all benefit from that!!!

Ross always wanted to please...whether it be parents, teachers, caregivers or tutors. But the thing that trips these kids up is how they misinterpret interactions when social demands increase once they become teenagers. As we all know, it's so much easier to get away with saying something inappropriate or acting in a way that's socially unacceptable when you're a toddler or in elementary school. Once you hit the teenage years, the perceptions amongst friends, students, teachers and adults have definitely changed and they are no longer as accepting and supportive as they had been in the earlier years. After all, there comes a time when it's just not cute any longer.

This was a period in Ross' childhood when Social Skills Training was vital. I guess if a child prefers not to socialize, it may not be as vital. But in Ross' case, everyone was his friend. So part of the Social Skills training was not just teaching Ross appropriate behaviors and "good manners", it was also teaching him the inappropriate behaviors or attitudes of kids who really didn't consider him to be a friend. And that's a tough pill for all of us. Ross will soon realize that oftentimes when kids aren't accepting, there's a great likelihood that they will mature into adults who aren't accepting.

So Ross began by attending Social Skills Group once a week with other children which was conducted in a clinical setting. After about six months, the consensus was that he was being used more as a role model for the other children in the group. While this was great to hear, we still needed to address the issues that were hanging him up in school amongst his classmates and friends. We eventually held Social Skills Group in our home with Ross' friends and one of the school psychologists. It kind of turned into a monitored get-together, if you will. We would sometimes take the boys miniature golfing or bowling and would just hang back and observe and then move in when Ross needed coaching or guidance. So rather than just leave Ross off on his own, for a year or two, he learned the give-and-take and nuances of friendship that hopefully will continue to help him nurture and sustain the friendships he's had since elementary school. He's very fortunate to be surrounded by a group of really good guys who accept Ross and all that he brings to the table!

So these rules were all somehow linked to situations that had arisen, challenges that we were confronted with, or just plain old inappropriate behaviors that Ross (as well as we, his parents) wanted to either isolate or extinguish.

Since those with autism are known to recall and draw upon past experiences, I thought it might be useful if Ross had these written rules to refer back to during his teenage years. My guess is that he has them memorized, that his initial reading of them stuck and, although he rebelled upon receipt, that he's drawn upon them in dicey situations when he had to call on that inner voice that so many teenagers choose to ignore, which sometimes leads to making the wrong choice.

Getting back to the 13 Rules...I wanted to call them the 13 Commandments, but Ross wouldn't allow that. We would recall them at bedtime when Ross said his prayers. After a while, Ross would just ask God to help him follow the rules....Amen.

Ashley's enthusiasm about Christmas and birthdays never really became contagious. Ross needed to work through a lot of the sensory overload issues that he was experiencing at a young age before that was possible.

Chapter 7

The Link between Court Reporting and Autism... is there one?

While I shouldn't even be delving into this subject, because I am certainly not licensed, wise enough, or the least bit educated in the field, the brain has always fascinated me...almost as much as human behavior. I just think that the brain in underrated. When I think about everything that Ross has had to be "taught" because he didn't learn from his environment...and the overload that we've put his brain through...it's no wonder that he's the amazing young guy that he is. I often think about how different Ross' brain is from mine. While he can blow me away reciting facts and figures, he can also blow me away when I give him a three-step instruction and he has to have me repeat it. From a very young age, I've always told Ross this, "Your brain is amazing; however, you do not want to clutter it." (Clutter does not fit into Ross' world;

everything has its place.) "So please promise me that you'll not clutter it with useless information (i.e., addresses and phone numbers of those whom you'll never have to contact; dates and times that really would be of no interest to the general population (Ross can remember that on Father's Day, June 6, 1995, he was sick and couldn't enjoy the day) so as to leave room for your studies and important information, as well as fun facts that will keep you in touch with the people you love."

Some days more than others I feel that I put my human brain through some rather superhuman, extremely complex functions in order to remain focused and alert in order to produce an accurate transcript. For those of you who have never had the pleasure of giving a deposition or testifying in court (a touch of sarcasm there!) and seeing the distant look on the court reporter's face, it's almost the look of autism. It's as if I'm looking "through" you and not "at" you. I can't speak for all court reporters, but when I'm in depositions I personally need to fixate on a person or object and literally zone out. But all the while, I am fully present and preparing to "will my brain and my fingers" to transmute the spoken word into text.

I went back to school to become a court reporter shortly before Ross was diagnosed. I had been with Bell Atlantic for 18 years. After I had determined that Ross would require a little more than Ashley had as a toddler (although never dreaming we'd be faced with autism) and not having the luxury of being a stay-at-home mom, I researched the court reporting profession and felt it might be a good fit. While researching the field, one of the biggest perks was that I believed it would give me the flexibility I eventually would need as the mother of Ashley and Ross who were two years apart. So I accepted

Beating the Odds at Autism

one of the management buyouts that Bell Atlantic offered and off I went back to school for three years.

Well, hindsight is 20/20. At that time, I never, ever dreamed that ABA therapy would be in the cards and begin in our home, 40 hours a week, 7 days a week. My full-time position at Bell Atlantic would not have been conducive to this – as fulfilling a position as it was – it did require some traveling and after-hour attendance of Board Meetings, etc. Well, thankfully, for the three years I attended school at night, I was able to be there for the ABA sessions during the day when therapist after therapist would arrive at our home. I was also able to be there for the preschool program, coordination between our home program and the school day and transporting Ross to doctor visits, occupational therapy and social skills' sessions as well.

I remember like it was yesterday, pulling away from our home for my 40-minute drive to school four nights a week for three years, many times Ross tantruming upon my escape. I would "allow" myself to cry the entire way there and "allow" myself to cry the entire way home. However, while in class, I was the attentive, stoic student! Looking back, the three years of intensive schooling provided a release, a respite for me, from the turmoil that had turned our once peaceful home into a "hotel of sorts" with a revolving door through which teachers, tutors, therapists, psychologists and consultants would enter and exit seven days a week. All we were missing was a valet out front to shuffle cars!

That being said, I do feel that I had chosen the best professional placement for what lie ahead. This choice has also allowed me to develop and nurture client relationships that have become like family...lifelong friendships that I cherish because they've been through Ross' entire journey with me...but then again, Ross is just beginning!

Now, getting back to the amazing brain. When you consider the key cognitive skills: attention (sustained, selective and divided), memory (long- and short-term) logic and reasoning, auditory processing, visual processing and processing speed...where do we begin, since all of these areas are affected in a child with autism. I would have to say that auditory processing, which is the most important skill a child must master in order to learn to read, was our greatest challenge. I sometimes wonder if we'll ever be able to "bridge the gap" which Ross compensates for so adeptly in his daily life. Although his long-term memory enabled him to read and recall facts at an extremely early age, the gap in comprehension caught up in time. And then his deficits in attention and short-term memory contributed to a slower processing speed, which is often seen as a major component in ADHD-type behaviors as well.

So, I've said this to teachers over Ross' years of schooling...and I hope I don't offend any teaching professionals who dedicate their careers to educating our children...academics, kind of, took a back seat in our goals for Ross. Yes, the intelligence could be (and most times) is at a very high level in these kids, but of what value is it if they can't sit in a classroom without being disruptive, if they can't participate in the social benefits of being in a school setting, and if they can't generalize their knowledge to become independent members of society. In other words, our goal for Ross was for him to be as well-rounded, independent and as diverse as possible. While there is rarely a classic diagnosis of autism without "overlapping" diagnoses, in Ross' case OCD creeps in every now and then, as well as ADD. So you find yourself not just dealing with the classic autistic stereotypical behaviors, you're also dealing with the focus issues that go along with ADD and the obsession and compulsion issues that go along with OCD. It's quite a cocktail!

Now, we could have allowed Ross to obsess over high-interest subjects and sound like a little Einstein, or we could limit his talk time on those high-interest subjects, and that's what we chose to do. Once again....I'm overusing this word...as "militaristic" and insensitive as it may sound, if you want to minimize the behaviors that will "overtake" their lives, you really need to police their activities at a young age.

Here's an example...how annoying would it be if you were out to dinner with someone and they monopolized the entire conversation with their sole hobby? We tried to teach reciprocal conversation...as mundane as it was at times...with statement/ comment/statement. What this meant was, during therapy sessions we would have him pick conversation starters that were not necessarily obsessions of his, which made it much more challenging. We would then attempt to generalize these one-minute conversations at the dinner table, in the car, or while swinging on the swings. It was our attempt at teaching Ross to become reciprocal, not only in his conversations but also in his conversation topics. We were teaching him to think of a comment even in conversations that weren't necessarily of interest to him. A very creative activity around our dinner table was "high and low." We would take turns while having dinner as a family talking about the highs and lows of our day. This helped with recall, sharing and listening. I'm certain that some typically-developing kids could benefit from this activity which

59

would also help their parents learn more about what went on in school that day!

Do you get the idea that too much of anything is not good? That kind of sums it up. You work toward a goal; achieve the goal; and then sometimes you have to pull back because it will just run out of control. Ugh! Very frustrating, yet intriguing. It just makes you wonder about the human brain.

There are times in my career as a court reporter that I have been required to take down anywhere from 225 to 275 words per minute. This requires "storing/holding" the testimony in my brain until, as I said earlier, I can "will my brain and my fingers" to complete the task. I've often thought that this must be similar to what Ross encounters in everyday conversation and, of course, in the classroom. Since he requires that extra processing time, I imagine that he's "storing/holding" the verbal command, instruction or just everyday banter until he's able to respond or comment or complete the task.

I've also had an attorney turn to me and say, "Can you please read back her last answer?" And I am certain I've given the attorney that blank stare that Ross has given myself and others oh-so-often...that is, until I can eventually complete the action of my fingers getting the testimony from my brain to my writer. Then I can respond to his or her request. I believe that this is the delay we witness in exchanges with our kids and also in their response to instructions or requests. They just need that extra time to process...and it's much easier if no interruption follows. I am fine if the attorney doesn't fire away with the next question; as I'm sure Ross is okay if the teacher doesn't give a two-step instruction or assignment.

So I, especially in my profession, feel that I have more sensitivity to what our children encounter in their everyday lives. I'm curious to see if Ross feels there are any similarities...

Ross' thoughts:

I don't know how my brain compares to my mom's, but I do know that I am so smart that I could read about 10 books in a month, especially with reading novels in school and reviewing the guides in order for me to be prepared for quizzes or tests. Some novels that I read in school interest me, like I can pretend I'm one of the main characters or the narrator that tells readers about his or herself in stories. I don't really have too many obsessions about them because it's for school, but there are certain books I enjoy reading and I obsess about them a little.

Most of the time, I read books and articles about sports and other things that interest me deep down inside my mind, which my mom would be afraid that I would have a little bit of OCD over them and it will clutter my mind, which will not happen because I save room in my enormous brain for other important things, like in school, besides reading, including math, computer skills and other subjects that I focus on. I always want to spend time watching sports, completing my school work and studying. And I basically talk about those things with most of my friends, especially with my girlfriend at this time, because she has stuff in common with me that we both like to talk about, like sports and other things that we're interested in.

For example, when there's a Young Life meeting on a Monday night and there's sports on to watch that night, I don't go to those meetings. Now, while I'm not at Young

Life meetings, some people kind of miss me for not keeping in touch with them and they probably think I'm a little obsessed with watching sports.

On the other hand, my dad does some things that drive me a little bit nuts that he might be a little bit obsessed about, like singing and whistling. I understand why he does those things during his spare time, mainly to release his stress. Sometimes I tell him that he's quite obsessed about singing and whistling. My sister has also been obsessed about going on the computer we shared and not giving me a chance to go on ever since she was in fifth grade. Thankfully now that she's in college she has her own Mac.

I can't imagine who else I know has OCD right at this time but I'm sure there are a few people. And I would never want to ask or tell others if I believe they have obsessions with things, because I think that would be rude. I'm certain I'm not the only one in my group of friends with OCD, though.

I wish I never had OCD my whole entire life so that I could alternate my interests. I would have liked to learn by talking to certain people about different things that we were both interested in and not doing the same things all my life. It drives me nuts when my mom tells me that my OCD is really showing through or when she lets me know about things that I'm obsessed with. I never want to think about having OCD, even though I have good taste in things that I'm interested in. I'm just glad I'm me. While I have really good interests, most of them relate to me, like sports, because I watch and play them also.

I think it would be better if people could just have their interests, but not to the level of OCD in their lives.

Beating the Odds at Autism

It's evident how Ross became "comfortable in his own skin" over the years.

Chapter 8

The Gift of Acceptance

I believe that acceptance is one of the greatest gifts that I can give another person...

Let's face it, being the parent of a child with special needs is just this...you receive the diagnosis...you kick into action mode, educate yourself, develop relationships with the right professionals, surround yourself with people who are on the cutting edge of new therapies, and give your child the best of the best at whatever the cost...you just do it. It's much like the 90/10 Rule. That's the easy part.

The difficult part comes when you need to send this child out into our world and expect that other human beings will afford your child the same patience, understanding and respect that you've provided since their birth. This is difficult because, if you're like me, you expect to be treated the way that you treat others. Well, who hasn't been disappointed when we expect maybe a little too much and others don't step up to the plate. As I said, this is the difficult part, especially when it involves your child with autism.

We've all been in the company of someone with a physical challenge that requires a wheelchair, crutches, etc. What hopefully happens is society kicks in and gives that person a little extra time, offers them their seat and just shows a little extra courtesy and compassion. I often thought, wouldn't it be nice if we treated everyone this way. Well, when it comes to the guise of autism, here comes the real challenge, especially when it comes to other children. Our children are big and strong; or pretty and sweet, and most have no outward signs saying: Hey, world, I may need a little extra time to get through the jungle gym, process what you're asking me to do, or complete the task before me. So, therefore, it's a free pass for others to judge and misjudge and just generally disrespect. I've always said that high-functioning autism especially is a double-edged sword.

I never wanted Ross to receive preferential treatment because of his autism, and neither did he. So what I had to do was toughen up and be a big enough girl to say: You know, Linda, if you don't understand autism and all of its idiosyncrasies, how do you expect others to? Well, that may be, but how do you account for sheer disrespect? You don't. But once again, you have to consider the fact that others are being rude and disrespectful to your kid because of who "they are" and not because your kid has autism. And, I believe, this is a life lesson. I certainly know adults who do not treat others with respect and they don't apologize for the way they are. What I've tried to teach Ross (and Ashley because she has felt the hurt over the years watching

---

others interact with Ross as well) is just this...when I'm dealing with a difficult person, I try to emotionally take a step back and acknowledge that this isn't personal (or in Ross' case, a spinoff of the fact that he has autism.) I remind myself that the other person's behavior is part of their makeup and agenda and it doesn't necessarily require me to respond to it, so I generally don't. This in no way suggests that I don't expect my kids to stand up for themselves and advocate for themselves and others, it just suggests that they don't need to feed the other person's behavior by a negative response. Even though I've never made excuses for Ross' behavior or inappropriate behavior, as there was always a consequence, others may be battling something as well. And I've always found when I treat those difficult people with respect and compassion, it kind of diffuses the situation and they become a little more patient...sometimes. It's just really difficult when it comes to your child.

On the flip side, you will encounter so many situations where society just embraces your child and people continually amaze you with their understanding and sensitivity, especially in social situations that are stigmatizing. Their human compassion just kicks in and makes the situation right. I can think of times during Ross' childhood where I was overwhelmed by these young kids who displayed acts of sensitivity and compassion when it could not have been taught.

I'd like to share with you an email that I sent to my family and friends, teachers and tutors, after dropping Ross off to his first official Washington Township High School 2007 JV football practice in the summer of '07.

———◆———

08/15/07 at 11:47 a.m., I wrote:

"I just wanted to take a minute to share a highlight of my summer with all of you who have, in some way, played a role in making it happen.

I dropped Ross off for his first official WTHS 2007 football practice yesterday at 7 a.m. and lost it. Maybe it was because the night before we had watched World News Tonight which highlighted a camp for autistic children...a camp where, for the first time, parents were hearing their child speak a word. (A pediatric neurologist at Jefferson Hospital said Ross would never speak; teach him sign language.) A camp where these children got one-on-one interaction (that same one-on-one interaction that many of his tutors so painstakingly carried him up to his room seven days a week to give.) A camp where these children were rewarded and recognized for quelling the anxiety they felt about having to put themselves in a swimming pool for the first time (recognition that many teachers/tutors/therapists have given inside the school setting and outside the school setting because they knew it took fortitude on Ross' part to quell that anxiety without medication.)

I watched him as he got his duffle bag out of my car, swung it over his big, broad shoulders, held his head high, gave me a wink, and walked onto the field with so many big, strong jocks. I just sat there and thought about the strong constitution and self-confidence it must take to be able to do that, especially in Washington Township where we have so many outstanding athletes competing, private trainers, etc.

In closing, I pulled away and thanked God for "blessing

Beating the Odds at Autism

me with a child like Ross"...and then I laughed to myself and thought, I'll bet God never heard that prayer before...actually being thanked for sending a parent a child with a lifelong challenge! But Ross has changed my life in so many amazing ways and I have all of you to thank for that, because don't think for one minute that you haven't played an integral part in it!"

Warmest regards,
Linda

———◆———

I chose to include this email to, not only reflect back on Ross' three years of high school football, but to mention the support and patience of the entire football team...yes, total jocks...as well as amazing coaches and staff. Ross was "part of the team" and I feel he was treated as part of the team because he never slacked off. He was present for every weight-training session, as grueling as they were, and for every practice in full uniform in 90+ temperatures in August. When others recognize the commitment and stick-to-itiveness that Ross displays, there's a feeling of acceptance...and that's all Ross really wants out of life...to be accepted and treated like "one of the crowd." So three years later and two TDs later, Ross will be playing Varsity ball next year as a Senior and loving it! I believe as a society we need to move beyond our egocentric world view toward a fresh, new perspective that accepts and embraces all human beings equally.

And once again I go back to what I prayed for when we got the diagnosis. I never prayed for a cure; I prayed for the wisdom to understand and make the right choices

The Gift of Acceptance

for Ross until he is able to make those choices on his own. And when that time comes, I will retreat and not make those choices for him, but gently guide his thought process in order to come to those decisions with clarity. And to this day, I still believe that acceptance is one of the greatest gifts I can give another person...

Here are Ross' thoughts...

I was so happy when everyone on the sideline and the bleachers cheered me on and congratulated me when I scored those two TDs as you just read. I felt like a hero like from a constellation or somewhere.

As I was saying, I always want to treat others how I want to be treated, especially with women. For example, when I request girls for dates politely and they have plans, they postpone them which makes me feel good and pleased. In fact, when I'm out with my friends eating and everything, I treat them or sometimes they'll treat me, and I always ask them, "Are you sure? It's my treat." It's the best way to treat others the same as you want to be treated. Not everyone with autism is angry or anything; however, they get that way when others debate or whatever. I was like that a long time ago. I have been learning right from wrong and it is getting much easier for me as I am maturing. I want the world to be a better place.

Well, because I work hard and everything, I sometimes get stressed and my tone raises a little bit; therefore, I would need to relax for a short while. Anyway, I've been busy a lot with football, landscaping, and hanging with my friends. I just wish everyone would treat me how I want to be treated, but it is not happening.

Beating the Odds at Autism

There are some people who treat me the wrong way; such as, putdowns and saying stupid things, etc. But I am not like that and will not change because of other people.

We had Challenge Day at our high school. Every student at Challenge Day talked about what was wrong with their lives and everything, and everyone cried but me. Because overall, my life, it is all good! Nevertheless, I had to say something about something bad that had happened to me. But Challenge Day was fun for me because we played some games and we partied and everything. And I hugged some people which I like to do (well, only women, honest to God!) I have some lady friends as my good and best friends, and we treat each other the way we want to be treated. Now that's a "Gift of Acceptance!" It is what I need 24/7/365.

Note: At the Washington Township High School Football Banquet in January, 2010, Ross was presented with the ***Ross Burns Spirit Award*** which will be given to a player each year in Ross' name. At the presentation of the award, Coach Wechter expressed that Ross' spirit and energy is contagious amongst the players and that, if he was ever having a bad day, when Ross walked onto the field it changed!

The Gift of Acceptance

Being chased by Dad in Lahaska, PA and driving a speed boat on Marco Island, FL – always attempting to "live in the moment."

Beating the Odds at Autism

Chapter 9

---◆---

Living in the Moment

Okay...those of you who know me well know all too well that I occasionally walk to the beat of a different drummer. In this crazy world, I've learned to live in the moment, and that's my excuse. While I try not to ruminate about the past or worry about things that haven't happened yet or that I can't change, I do try to learn from things that didn't quite turn out the way I would have liked and move on. I've tried to teach this mindset to both of my children and hope that they've adapted, even a piece of it, and I think they have.

Now, how might this apply to the mind of an individual with autism, you might ask. Well, Buddhists call our minds "monkey minds" because we flit from one thought to another just like monkeys swing from trees. Just as I tell Ross not to "clutter his mind" with useless information, I've always tried to have him focus on the present...and I mean focus, which is a task in and of itself

---

for him. Telling him to be aware of his thoughts, but not have his thoughts control him. Thoughts are only thoughts; they cannot make you do anything you don't want to do. I'm sure this was not an easy concept to grasp, especially at a young age, for either child. But what I would do in a very matter-of-fact way, was model just how I was living in the present. The more I modeled; the more they picked up on it and reciprocated.

They would laugh at me when they were younger and I would get them up from the couch while watching a movie to come outside in their pajamas to look at the stars on a clear night or how the full moon was lighting up the sky. Now while driving in the car, one or both will say to me: Hey, Mom, look at that beautiful sky...or the unusual shape of those clouds...or the way the sun is setting behind the trees...and I enjoy a private chuckle. Just by incidental teaching, I think they've come to realize that when you work so hard at "life" you have to reward yourself with the little "perks of life" and be aware enough to not let anything pass you by. And it doesn't take an enormous amount of money or exotic islands, it just takes awareness of all the beauty that surrounds us.

Mindfulness, in my opinion, enables you to be more accepting of your weaknesses while all the while raising your self-esteem. I think if you're present and aware in the here and now, you're less impulsive and reactive to situations. And for you parents, you know all too well that there is no "filter" with our children. While impulsivity has its time and place...and I love spontaneity...it doesn't serve the autistic child well in a classroom setting or out in public places. You know, all of that creative energy that we work tirelessly to pull out of them, we then have to curb and try to teach a proper time and place for expressing it. How conflicting this must seem to a child with autism. But once we can teach awareness, it not only helps with impulsivity, but they become more aware of their body and the appropriateness or inappropriateness of their self-stimulatory behaviors. I will even go so far as to say awareness can help with "stimming" (self-stimulatory behavior; such as, rocking, hand-flapping, grimacing) as well as stimming on certain foods and problems with attention. We would make Ross "accountable" for his behaviors. We taught him self-monitoring techniques, and that is nothing more than awareness. People who are mindful can hear negative feedback or corrective criticism and not feel threatened or insulted. In a way, it helps reduce that defensiveness that comes along with curbing those inappropriate behaviors. It's almost like Ross was protective of them...of course, because the self-stimulatory behaviors felt good to him.

When you are mindful, you are more aware of how you interpret what's going on in your mind at all times. For children with autism, there's a lot going on in their minds. You're also more aware of how you react to what's happening in your mind. If there's a lapse between what's going on in your mind, how you interpret it, and how you react to it, there's a chance that you'll make the right choice...and not the impulsive, reactive one, because it won't be an emotional choice. Your self-control is increased when you're mindful; you are able to monitor and control your behavior. And there are many of us who can benefit from this when interacting with others.

Now, many of you may be saying, sure, this sounds great but how do we teach this to children with autism. Well, it goes back to one basic principle...breathe. We taught Ross the art of relaxation and breathing techniques and when and how to apply them at a young

---

Living in the Moment

age. When you're focusing on your breathing, you have no choice but to bring yourself into the present. And your breath is always there with you. What a powerful tool...not magical...just powerful and effective. And the beautiful thing is you never, ever have to worry about leaving the house without it!

We actually had "STOP" cards (index cards) which his shadow (classroom aide) at school would flash when she anticipated an outburst or meltdown. He would read the card, stop, breathe, and make a better choice. And, of course, he would be immediately rewarded for making that better choice. And when I say immediate, I don't mean he would be allowed to eat a candy bar in class; however, he would be told that when he got home from school he had earned an extra 20 minutes on Nintendo, which he never had free access to. Nintendo, TV and computer were all "privileges" that Ross worked for and was also consequenced with by losing time to use them. There has been no excess in Ross' life...and I know that that's why he'll never take anything for granted.

I think it might be helpful for those of you with young children to hear about how we "taught" this self-monitoring, starting at home and then eventually working it into Ross' school day. As you know, you always have target behaviors that you're working on. So these would be the behaviors that he's monitoring. Start with one or two and add as he or she becomes more comfortable and confident and honest in their monitoring. One of the really tough self-stimulatory behaviors for Ross was bringing his hands to his face. It wasn't just the fact that this made him stand out, and Ross never wanted to stand out and be different from the other kids, but he would make a facial grimace (which I've told him over the years turned my beautiful little boy's face into a face that was unrecognizable to me.) We actually caught it on tape to show him how he looked when he brought his hands up and grimaced. He would do this when excited, nervous, stressed and at other various times just because it felt good.

So we would start with two or three-minute intervals. We removed all the language from it, which also removed the emotion. To tell Ross, "Don't put your hands up and make that face" would make Ross want to do it more. Yes, crazy as it sounds. Many children with autism crave attention; albeit negative at times. Ross also would catch himself when doing it and...since the "awareness" was there...it was a perfect opportunity to extinguish or minimize this learned behavior. And this was because Ross didn't want to stand out. I don't want anyone to be offended or feel that we set out to change everything about Ross. There are many parents out there who choose not to inhibit their children, and I applaud that. There are also many teens and adults reading this who enjoy continuing what feels good to them, and I say "go for it." We kind of let Ross lead us along some of the way. And when you listen to your child tell you over and over again that he doesn't want to be different, then you'll go to the ends of earth to help him feel like one of the crowd. Ross is the one that had the strong constitution to want to change certain things...he had the tough job...we were just there to guide him with strategies.

Getting back to the self-monitoring...we would set a timer for two or three-minute intervals. This was initially at home. Ross would have a sheet with a timetable on it in front of him. He would be engaged in another activity, which could be; watching TV, playing Nintendo, doing homework. He would put a checkmark on the sheet every time he allowed himself to stim. If he had no checkmarks and the timer went off, he earned extra minutes doing the activity of his choice, or going out for ice cream (in Ross' case it was usually cappuccino!) or staying up an extra 15 minutes. This eventually moved to more than one behavior, longer intervals, into the school setting, at public functions...the sheet turned into an index card which he could stick in his pocket...you get the picture. It works; it sticks; and it's something they don't outgrow. But remember, this doesn't come without awareness.

For me, awareness helps you to be more thankful...thankful for the little things...maybe that one behavior that you helped your child eliminate. And when you're thankful, it's more difficult to ruminate on the shortfalls of yesterday or dwell on the challenges of tomorrow. You're in the present and just thankful for what your child accomplished TODAY. As I mentioned in the preface, I've oftentimes said to some of my closest friends, with all the sadness in my life, I'm not sad...and that's because when you're living in the moment and feeling thankful, sadness is a conflicting emotion.

Now I'll let you hear from Ross and how he's learned to live in the moment!

I know no matter what I do, whether I'm excited about things or if I get frustrated about things, I shouldn't bring my hands up near my face or do anything else that may make me look silly. I've only done that when I was younger, but now I'm rarely doing that stuff as I'm getting older. But sometimes, when anyone in my family is about to have a discussion with me about something I did wrong, I kind of get "stiffed" and bring my hands up near my face. That is usually the toughest time for me to use self-control, when I have discussions with my family, which I really find frustrating. I don't usually do it anymore when things do not go my way or aren't fair to me.

Sometimes it has been difficult for me to not stim, but as I get older, I do stim less. Sometimes it just happens when I'm excited about things or when I'm angry or frustrated about things. I'm really sure that exercising and heavy work, like landscaping, helps me stop being all emotional in those kind of ways.

When I focus on one thing and I forget to do another, that is also a time when I stim. Like when I talk about things with my family, like what lessons I need to learn, if I make those same mistakes about two or three times, I get all emotional about it. Therefore, I get told about mistakes that I've been making and I freak out, and it is tough for me to use self-control. I try to make sure I don't make the same mistakes over and over, to not be put to shame.

It has been getting better for me to stim less, except when people raise their voices at me or when things don't go my way, especially when it's not fair. If I didn't stim at all, there wouldn't be situations for me to try to use self-control. But if it still happens, I work on it and figure out some strategies that I've learned over the years.

Ashley always there to guide...
Ross always there to listen...

Chapter 10

Ashley's Chapter

Hmm...so now it's time for my chapter. Well, my name is Ashley. I am Ross' amazing, beautiful, intelligent, older sister...ha-ha, just kidding. But this book is all about him! I had to make my chapter somewhat about me!

So, my brother Ross...where should I begin? Ross has been a major part of my life, and I of his, ever since his birth when I was two. Ross is one funny guy, probably one of the funniest people I've ever spent time with. In addition to being witty, he's also smart, kind-hearted, loving and compassionate. He is the best brother I could ever have asked for. I wouldn't trade him for anything in the world (well, maybe free designer clothes for life)! But I will say that growing up with a sibling with autism isn't always easy, and as for you siblings reading this, I know you understand that all too well. Ross wasn't always so much fun to be around and hang out with. There were some very difficult times growing up...and very painful times as his sister...but I know now that we had to go through those difficult times to get to where we are as a family today. And as I said, I wouldn't have it any other way.

Let's start at the beginning. My experience with my brother Ross has been a long, difficult, but rewarding journey...and I do say journey because of this. When you're living in a household with an autistic sibling, autism is always the topic of conversations, disagreements, suggestions...well, it's pretty much all that's talked about. It's either that "they" had a good day, or "they" had a bad day, but it's always the main topic. We got to a point where "it" became known as "the A word" for short. My mom believed from a very young age that, although Ross was non-verbal, he was like a sponge and soaking in much of what was going on around him. She felt that although his expressive language was delayed or virtually non-existent, that his receptive was not as affected. I think, to be honest, she just didn't really want to take a chance that his self-esteem would be affected by hearing the word autism being thrown around along with the negative connotations at that time. I think early on she probably thought that he needed to be "labeled" in order to receive the services so necessary to his learning and success; however, a label is just a label. Let's face it, every one of us could fit into a neat little category and receive a label.

I remember listening to meetings around my kitchen table, which took place every other week, year in and year out, with Ross' consultant and tutors and therapists, as well as teachers and my mom, just brainstorming and bouncing things off of each other. I remember at times when hearing them discuss behaviors or challenges, my mom would say, is it really "the A word" or is it just typical "kid stuff"? I think my mom was happy at times when that typical "kid stuff" would surface, as it meant that we were doing something to peel through the layers of autism. So really, "the A word" was the main focus in my house for many years of my childhood.

Fifteen years ago when my brother was being diagnosed, autism was not talked about nearly as much as it is today. When my brother was born, he was not unlike many other newborns. He was a healthy weight at birth, born by C-section, as was I. He ate, slept and smiled occasionally, as I can remember, as my mom would let me hold his bottle and feed him...just as big sisters do, right? It wasn't until he was a toddler that my mom had noticed something was wrong. She had gone to the library at the time and researched developmental delays and, in her mind, autism seemed to fit. (How times have changed, now we'd be on the internet.) Many of the signs were similar to what Ross was exhibiting. She then went to our pediatrician and shared her thoughts. Although he told her that he had never thought about Ross possibly being autistic, when a Mother told him something was wrong, he trusted in her.

So now it was time to start the diagnosis process. The first recommendation our pediatrician made was to have his hearing checked. Now, I didn't think that this could be a problem, but what did I know, I was only five at the time. Ross knew exactly when Sesame Street was on TV, even from upstairs. Or if he was asked to go to the playground, he would come running. Needless to say, Ross' hearing tests came back just fine. On to Step 2...

My parents then started evaluations with teams of developmental specialists. Remember, 15 years ago, autism was not anywhere nearly as "popular" as it is now. Nowadays, when the word autism is brought up, whether I'm at school, amongst friends, or out and about, I find that someone has a connection with autism, somehow; some way. Since there is no real "test" for autism, observation by a specialist is very important. During this evaluation process, the dreaded words were spoken: Ross was autistic. Right then, although I didn't quite understand what autism was, I knew enough that Ross' life would dramatically start to change. Little did I know that my life was going to be changed dramatically as well.

Of course, as I said, as a child I didn't understand what autism was. I had absolutely no idea. However, I knew that my little brother was different. Starting from the time I was about, I'd say, kindergarten age, I can remember knowing he was different. I had a friend say to me, "Why is your brother not like everyone else"? How do I answer that? When you're six years old and trying to figure out that question for yourself, it makes it pretty hard to give an explanation to another six-year-old. In my experience, siblings of autistic children really grow up quickly and mature faster than others. Looking back, it's really easy to see why.

Throughout my childhood years growing up with Ross, I felt like I kicked into mother mode when my mom was not around. When we would be out playing in the neighborhood or riding on the school bus together, I felt as though I always needed to be right by his side, whether or not that was where my friends were. We would always go out to play and I wouldn't even be able to enjoy myself. I felt as though the whole time I would be watching him, making sure he wasn't getting hurt, or watching his behaviors and observing if he was acting appropriately around the other kids. If he started to stim or have a tantrum, I knew just how to handle it, even at such a young age. This came from having 30 to 40 hours a week of ABA done in our home from the time he was diagnosed. I was a big part of this therapy and served as a peer model to teach reciprocal play, waiting your turn, etc. I'm sure many of the siblings reading this can definitely relate. I loved my brother so much and at times I felt like he was one of my best friends. But there were countless times that I had to explain to people why he acted differently or had to help Ross understand how to play a certain game that other kids picked up on their own. I was willing to do anything in the world for him in order to make his life easier.

While growing up with an autistic brother the thing that actually bothered me the most was how ignorant other people could be. I remember getting stares and comments when going out in public or even in church...yes, church. We were Roman Catholic at the time and I became an altar server in the third grade. My brother, who was always very in tune with his religion, wanted to follow in my footsteps. So there we were on the same altar serving team with me as his guide up on the altar every Sunday. I remember how proud my mom and dad were. They would sit in the first pew every Sunday, but I could see the anxiety on their faces, just hoping that he could keep it together because it was something he wanted to do. There were so many times where he'd be close to a meltdown because of overstimulation in our huge church. The choir...the bells...the congregation in prayer...but he wanted to do it so we taught him strategies which enabled him to not "melt down" up on the altar in front of the entire congregation. It took all the strength I had not to curse people off or knock them out (and I am the least violent person ever, I promise!) but I just couldn't believe how rude and unsympathetic people could be...churchgoers no less. Although, I always told my mom that people are not just targeting Ross because he's autistic, that's just the way they are to everyone. There will always be people that are just plain mean. In the end, I feel badly for them. They never get to experience the joy and awesomeness (I know; I know, it's not a real word) that Ross brings to everyone around him. And my life is definitely better from having had firsthand experience of his "awesomeness."

When we were young, I felt as though I always had to look after Ross. I would try to teach him whatever I could. It was not always easy, especially during the early years. Whether we were watching TV, playing a board game, or just spending time around our house, I would try to ask him questions and get him involved in any way that I could. I don't even think that I realized I was doing it. I just loved him so much and wanted him to be part of my world and the world around him. I would help the tutors during his ABA drills. We called them "drills" because the ABA program can appear as though the tutor is the drill sergeant and the student is the cadet. The tutor gives the command: Come here. Ross then has to stop whatever he's doing and come over to begin the drill without complaining. A drill could be anything from teaching a self-help skill to identifying a proper noun to modeling turn-taking. I remember I made idiom cards because Ross was taking idioms a little too seriously. When someone said: It's raining cats and dogs, Ross would run over to the window and look for animals falling from the sky!

Another funny thing I remember was putting on a Beanie Baby Christmas Show. We would set up the family

Beating the Odds at Autism

room and set up a stage. All of our Beanie Babies were collected and we would put on a show. It was really hilarious. (I really wish I could insert a video clip right here.) We would make fake tickets and hand them out to our family members. I would guide Ross on which characters to use; however, sometimes he would put his own spin on things. It was a real bonding experience for us. I remember the Christmas after 9/11 we incorporated NYC and the Twin Towers into our show as a tribute to the victims of 9/11. He really "got it" because our parents had taken us to Ground Zero a few weeks after September 11th to light candles and have Ross experience the devastation firsthand. They always wanted him to have the same experiences that I did as a child...both happy and sad.

I remember on vacations at the beach I would teach Ross how to make sandcastles or drag him out in the ocean with me. Beach time was always very relaxing for Ross, whether it was the feel of the sand or the sound of the ocean. Relaxing until a wave would knock down our sandcastles or someone would walk over the endless train tracks he would carve in the sand...then a major meltdown would occur. But all in all, he really was like my best friend. I will always remember those fun times along with plenty of others that we've shared growing up.

Whenever I think of Ross, I think of the struggles he's had as a child and how far he has truly come. It is so hard to believe that he is a young man now. I am so amazed at the way Ross has matured and has really learned to think for himself. I was talking with my friend Amanda (who has been a big part of our family forever now and has had nothing but respect for Ross) a couple days ago when we called Ross into the room. She had tried to make a joke with him when he gave a nervous smile and chuckled a little. That is one thing I find really funny about autism...Ross only sees the world in black and white. He is extremely literal. Ross sensed that she had made a joke, but could not fully process it. He had known to give a smile though, which to him (and to me) was a sign that he got what was going on. He then proceeded to tell us that he had a date planned for the following night and that he would be using a coupon on this date since he wanted to try to save money! I am actually updating this as Ross is dating, yet again, another girl. It's pretty sad, but I really think he goes out more than I do. He definitely has better luck in relationships! He really just cracks me up every day. It's crazy that I now have to discuss his love relationships rather than helping him to complete a task independently.

Now that I have shared my experiences about my brother, I want to reach out to all of the siblings who are living with autism day in and day out, since we share a special bond. When my brother was diagnosed with autism, I felt so alone. I felt as though I was the only kid that had a brother who was autistic. As for today, autism is much more prevalent. There are many hard times growing up with an autistic sibling and you won't always have friends or another sibling to share things with. It's especially hard to vent to people at a young age. I definitely kept a lot to myself and learned to rely mainly on "just me." I know it was very hard for me to watch things that go on at school, at the playground, or on the bus when no one else is watching. One thing it has taught me is to always stand up when I see an injustice. Not just for those who are challenged in one way or another, but for people in general.

Now for the hard part...having most of the attention on your sibling isn't the best feeling in the world. Now,

Beating the Odds at Autism

don't get me wrong, I have two of the most supportive parents in the world, but sometimes no one can understand how you are feeling besides another sibling of an autistic child. I can remember one Christmas I broke down and started crying. Now, I know it sounds childlike, but I felt as if my brother had gotten all of the attention. I look back and think about how it was probably not the best way to react, but I just needed to let it out.

So, to all the siblings out there, just let out the frustration if it comes on! Go work out, go for a walk, or write it down or draw in a journal. Of course, my parents love me just as much as Ross, as do your parents. Sometimes it's just hard to see that from our perspective, especially if the majority of your brother or sister's therapy is taking place in the home. The most important thing I can say from this experience is be patient, kind, supportive, and loving. It will pay off big time in the end, not only for your sibling, but it will make you a better person as well.

The best thing to do, which helped me so much, is to surround yourself with good, supportive friends. I have the best friends in the entire world. My mother tells me that you attract people who are like yourself. Well, if so, I'm the luckiest person in the world. Many of them have been there for me since the beginning. If it wasn't for my friends, I would have felt very alone and wouldn't have had anyone to vent to. Also, it is good to get involved in activities dedicated to autism and become an advocate. For example, I have met so many other siblings of autistic children at Walks, fundraising dinners, seminars, and other charity events that my family has participated in. It is a great place to really connect with others that share similar experiences that we have had and will continue to have. As for becoming an advocate, I really feel like I have become one. I'm always sharing stories or giving advice about autism and have volunteered to participate in studies. I have also attempted to start up a Support Group for siblings but, I guess, it's difficult for parents to take this on while caring for their autistic child. I just wish they could realize how important it is to give their other children an opportunity for a release as well.

I hope that what I've shared can really help. I feel like giving all of you my phone number in case you ever want to talk about your experiences (but I probably wouldn't be able to get anything done.) With that being said, remember this, in the end it is **YOU** that will make such a huge impact on your brother or sister's development. **YOU** are one of their best friends and one day **YOU** and everyone around you will see how much **YOUR** love and kindness paid off!

For once in my life, I'm at a loss for words here...

Afterword

So...here we are four years beyond when I wrote the Preface for this book while on the beach when I was supposed to be working...and I'm still doing other things when I'm supposed to be working; i.e., writing this Afterword! I definitely know that the "apple doesn't fall far from the tree" when it comes to my son being easily distracted, but luckily I'm my own boss!

In all seriousness, I can remember like it was yesterday when I came home from the beach and shared the idea of writing a book with the kids (as they were actually both teenagers at the time.) When they became enthused and we talked about how this would be a great way of giving back, I added that I did not want it to become a burden. It had to be done from the heart and not interfere with living our lives, in order that we'd have more to write about. Well, that has become pretty evident since it has taken four years. I thought some of our readers might be interested in hearing where Ross is today, along with Ashley, so here goes...

In May of 2011, Ross completed his first year at Gloucester County College with a GPA of 3.7. He is planning to major in Civil Engineering with concentration in Land Surveying. He is able to work after obtaining his Associate's degree/Certificate in Land Surveying from the County College; however, he plans to see how he does this year and perhaps transfer to a University, such as LaSalle or Penn State, for his Bachelor's. He also mentioned to Ashley and I that he just "loves statistics" – and Ashley's response was "glad somebody does"! So he has also been exploring the world of statistics, which is so vast, and he can possibly apply it to the construction field or perhaps the world of casinos, if he decides to go on further for his Bachelor's degree.

I must tell you, though, that Ross has wanted to deal Blackjack or Craps at the Borgata (and only the Borgata) here in Atlantic City, NJ since he was in junior high school. He had "Casino Nights" at our home throughout middle school and high school. There were times when some of the parents would want to stay to have Ross "help them understand the game of Craps"! Another milestone (yes, milestone!) was when he got called down to the Principal's office in middle school for bringing cards to school and organizing poker games in the lunchroom.

College life has also been an adjustment for me; in that, Ross has to advocate for himself and I cannot be involved. Also, all of the supports vanish at the college level. The only accommodations are note-takers, which Ross declined, and remote testing (which he initially declined but once he found out he bombed a test purely because of the fact that he didn't finish, he elected to rethink the option next time around.) I believe it gives Ross a feeling of empowerment to have to think on his own and make his own decisions -- with the advice of his advisor, of course -- when choosing his courses, scheduling them, etc. He, by the way, is President of the Bowling Club, which keeps him involved with other students at the college and allows them to meet every Wednesday night at 9 throughout the school year.

Aside from the fact that every time I turn around Ross is either studying or doing a paper on his laptop, in his free time he enjoys working out at the gym, hanging out with friends to watch sports, as well as getting together with the guys to golf. Back when he was in high school, after trying out for the golf team both freshman and sophomore year, he finally made the team both junior and senior year. What's nice about it is that he can mature into the game of golf. He has many friends with whom he golfs so it was an all-around good choice. Although he played football in high school, I don't know too many 70-year-olds who still get together on the football field. He also enjoys reading on his Kindle, especially on the beach, eating out and going to sporting events. He's a huge Philadelphia Sports teams' fan (as I'm sure you picked up on in previous chapters), but has also gone to visit other stadiums in various states with his dad, which is something they plan on continuing.

Ross works with his dad in his landscaping business. The heavy work is an added benefit to Ross' sensory system, along with the fact that he appreciates the value of a dollar now that he's a working man. He's very money-smart, handles all of his own banking and has begun investing. Actually, next year his father plans to turn the business over to him while being there to accompany him on the larger landscaping jobs; however, leaving the lawn maintenance strictly to Ross. Ross is

95

Afterword

really looking forward to taking over the business while still in college.

And then there's Ross' love life which is quite colorful. He has had two long-term relationships; one lasting over a year. He has been both the one to break off a relationship (for very valid reasons in his mind) as well as being on the receiving end. He is very open-minded when it comes to different religions and nationalities, which makes me so pleased as a parent. He feels that he won't be ready for marriage for quite some time, because he would "find it hard to be faithful" (Ross will always tell you the truth) and doesn't feel at this time that he wants the awesome responsibility that comes with being a parent.

Now I come to my Ashley Nicole! She is now 21 and quite the poised young lady when she is required to be and quite the quirky kid that I remember when she's able to be! Since she was required to grow and mature at a much quicker pace than her friends because of her family situation, I welcome the times when she just lets her hair down and acts like a kid again.

Ashley began her senior year at Drexel University in September, 2011. She lives on campus, as University City is a fun place to be. Although we live in close enough proximity to commute, living on campus benefits her as far as the requirements of being a volunteer for various clubs and organizations within Drexel along with just having the true college experience.

In addition to carrying 18 credits, she also works part-time. She has been an ABA therapist since her junior year of high school and has acted as both a therapist and shadow with autistic children in their home programs and school settings since then. The feedback I've gotten is that she is a welcomed addition to any team of ABA therapists as well as the parents. I would assume that Ashley's "life experience" is a nice complement to the "book knowledge" of other therapists, and has to be such an added level of comfort to parents.

She will be well into her senior year at Drexel just about the time this book gets published. She is majoring in Psychology, plans on attending grad school and wants to eventually work with schizophrenics. Last spring she was inducted into the International Psychology Honor Society. She also participates in a research lab at the University and has been an active fundraiser and passionate (and vocal!) supporter of many causes.

Ash enjoys many of the things that other college kids do: hanging out with friends, eating out, shopping and music; music; music. Our home has rarely been without music; therefore, the kids have been exposed to just about every genre. Even though there's 30 years between us, Ash and I continue to expose each other to new artists and will attend concerts and arts/music festivals together every chance we get. (Although, to be honest, she did fall asleep when attending a Josh Groban concert together a few years back... but nonetheless, she went with me!)

In her free time (which she has very little of) she enjoys going out with friends, surfing, yoga, and hanging out with her brother and Sophia (her year-old Shih Tzu) who both bring much joy to her life.

As for me...Linda A. Burns...I am enjoying my 50th year on this earth, especially since I accomplished my goal of finalizing this book before Ross turned grey! My husband Bob and I will celebrate our 30th wedding anniversary in June of 2012 and I just celebrated the 10th anniversary of Infinity Court Reporting, LLC. I feel that I've managed to maintain a balance between my professional and personal worlds and I hope to continue doing what I'm doing for a long time to come. I feel that court reporting will be an ideal profession to mature into and my dream is to write the sequel to this book as I had begun this one...on the plane back from some exotic place while continuing to make memories.

In closing, my wish for every reader of our book is just this...that those parents of newly-diagnosed children will find Ross' story to be inspirational, compelling and perhaps the medicine you need to continue the fight; that those living with any challenge may flourish in a world of acceptance; and that those who are unaffected by any of life's struggles may find it in their heart to embrace differences in others and help them beat the odds at this crazy thing we call life.

Ross has grown increasingly more comfortable with public speaking. He recently addressed a class at Drexel University at the request of one of Ashley's Professors.

Afterword

Ross and one of his favorite girls...Sophia!

And having a drink at a bar on his first cruise...

Ross and his dad literally "hanging out" in Newfoundland and taking advantage of a "photo op" before Ross' High School Graduation ceremony in June of 2010.

Who knows what the future will hold for Ross...but one thing I do know is this...his joy comes from within, therefore, he will never look to something or someone to bring him happiness. His energy is infectious!

"To Do List" for Parents

I can reflect back to how overwhelming it was after getting the diagnosis. Even though you have your Child Study Team, doctors, psychologists and, hopefully, family and friends who are willing to do whatever is necessary, you need to feel some control over the hand you've just been dealt. I thought that this list might prove helpful (and I started with suggestions even before the definitive diagnosis is received.)

1. Listen to your instinct. Don't dismiss any behavior (whether it be viewed as odd, advanced for your child's age, or delayed for your child's age.) The key is early diagnosis; early intervention, so don't leave anything to chance.

2. Consult your pediatrician first. If he or she tells you to "wait it out," DON'T. Seek out another opinion and, if your child is of the preschool age, query his or her teacher, classroom aide, etc., for any valuable feedback/comments/observations. Make note of these to share at your first appointment.

3. Make the appointment. It may seem like it's in the distant future, which will be the case with a reputable practice. Again, keep a journal in the meantime. Keep data of any behavior that seems "odd" or "different" or "weird."

4. Once you receive the diagnosis, in all likelihood your first specialist will be a speech pathologist. Your second will be an occupational therapist. Your third

will (should) be a therapist with the appropriate training in sensory integration therapy.

5. I can't stress enough how important a therapist trained in sensory integration is in the overall "desensitizing" of your child to stimuli. I feel that this was the "missing link" in Ross' initial team of professionals. It wasn't until the 4th grade when I researched and sought out a therapist with this specialized training for Ross to treat with. It made a world of difference and, in my opinion, prevented him from having to go on medication for anxiety...realizing that this is a strong opinion. This is essential even if you're not seeing evidence of overstimulation. It's necessary to regulate the child's nervous system which is still developing in order to cope with, minimize or perhaps prevent SPD (Sensory Processing Disorder) or SID (Sensory Integration Disorder).

6. Once your child is "set up for success" with his or her team of therapists, you must bring social skills training into the mix, even at a young age. We found that participation in a social skills group which involved Ross' peers/friends was extremely beneficial. He was more "available" to the teaching and suggestions since he's always had the desire to "fit in" and what better way to teach reciprocal play/turn-taking than from your child's peers/friends.

7. Expose your child to everything. We never sheltered Ross. We gave him the ability to experience everything that Ashley did...from Scouts, to soccer, to bowling, to IMAX theaters, to live Broadway shows, to concerts, to airline flights, to speed boats to train

rides...I can go on and on and on. This helped, not only to desensitize Ross by providing him with coping mechanisms to deal with over-stimulating social events, but it also helped form his preferences in life.

8. Keep food journals. We never placed Ross on any of the restrictive diets that are proving to be very beneficial to some children at the time of this writing. There either wasn't enough research that had been done at the time, or we just didn't feel it was warranted at the toddler stage. Ross could have ended up with a very restrictive, not-very-nutritious diet; however, we motivated him to at least try new foods. He is now into health and fitness so that he counts calories and watches what he eats...because he would eat just about any food group (as long as the food wasn't served broken...yes, it's still all about the presentation!)

9. Encourage exercise. We all know how beneficial workouts can be; however, for a child on the spectrum, physical activity is crucial. If it becomes "part of life" they'll never know anything different!

10. And lastly, remember -- in between the tears, that is -- try to smile and bring humor to some of your days. As I said before, it's very difficult to feel defeated when you're finding a reason to smile.

"To Do List" for Parents

At one of our Annual Walks for Autism and spending a very special Mother's Day in Manayunk, PA.

Glossary of Terms

ABA – Applied Behavior Analysis

ADD – Attention Deficit Disorder

Antecedent to behavior - You'll often hear this referred to as ABC – *Antecedent* (what happened just before the undesirable behavior was exhibited) *Behavior* (the undesirable behavior) *Consequence* (the consequence of the undesirable behavior.)

ASD – Autism Spectrum Disorder

ASL – American Sign Language

ASDs – Autism Spectrum Disorders

EIRC – Educational Instructional Resource Center

Meltdown – an outburst, usually caused by excessive sensory stimulation

NT (or Neurotypical) - a term which the autistic community uses as a label for those who are not on the autistic spectrum

OCD – Obsessive Compulsive Disorder

PDD-NOS – Persuasive Developmental Disorder – Not Otherwise Specified – full criteria for autism not met.

Shadow – aide in school/social settings

SID – Sensory Integration Dysfunction

SPD – Sensory Processing Dysfunction

SSRI – Selective serotonin reuptake inhibitors – class of drugs typically used as antidepressants. Used for depression, anxiety.

Stim (or self-stimulatory behavior) – repetitive body movement, stimulates senses. Usually exhibited with concentration, excitement, et cetera.

Photography by
Dennis Kelly